WAVES AND BEACHES

WILLARD BASCOM, president of Ocean Science and Engineering, Inc., has been affectionately studying the motions of sea and sand since 1945. He is happiest walking at the water's edge, whether it be Japan or South Africa, Cape Cod or Tahiti.

Mr. Bascom was born in New York City in 1916 and attended the Colorado School of Mines. After working in half a dozen states as a miner and engineer he began his study of beaches as a research-engineer for the Waves Project at the University of California, first at Berkeley and then at the Scripps Institution of Oceanography. In 1952 he measured the waves produced by the first thermonuclear blast at Eniwetok. The following year he sailed as chief scientist on the *R. V. Baird* on oceanographic expedition "Capricorn" through the tropical Pacific, which stopped at the Gilberts, Fijis, Tonga, Societies, Tuamotus, and other island groups. He left the Pacific to join the staff of the National Academy of Sciences, organizing committees on amphibious operations, civil defense, meteorology, oceanography, and maritime research. His company is now making basic studies of a series of California beaches and prospecting for undersea diamonds on the coast of South West Africa.

Mr. Bascom served as a special consultant to the Rockefeller Brothers Special Study Group; as a member of Project Nobska, which conceived the Polaris missile; and as a United States delegate to the International Geophysical Year conferences in Europe on oceanography and atmospheric radioactivity. After nine months in Tahiti, where he wrote on

Polynesian history and measured long-period waves for the IGY, Mr. Bascom became science consultant to the CBS "Conquest" television series, representing the American Association for the Advancement of Science and the National Academy of Sciences. He has served as a member of the Atomic Energy Commission Plowshare Committee concerned with the peaceful uses of nuclear explosions and as a member of the AAAS Committee on Public Understanding of Science.

Willard Bascom is best known for his work in organizing the Mohole Project for the National Academy of Sciences. He directed the Project's Phase I, which early in 1961 drilled five holes in the sea floor under water twelve thousand feet deep, setting many drilling records, and first sampled the geologically mysterious "second" layer. This work showed how the interior "mantle" of the earth can, some day, be probed directly with drills. Extensive work with this exciting project led to his book *A Hole in the Bottom of the Sea* (Doubleday & Company, 1961).

Mr. Bascom has written or edited many pamphlets, papers, and books on the subject, including *Shoreline Atlas of the Pacific Coast of the U. S., Drilling Through the Earth's Crust, Experimental Drilling in Deep Water,* and *Design of a Deep Ocean Drilling Ship.* His articles have appeared in *Scientific American, Nature, Journal of Geology,* and *Transactions of the American Geophysical Union.* He also has lectured on the Mohole Project and the general subject of oceanography on many occasions here and in Europe. Mr. Bascom lives in Washington.

WAVES AND BEACHES

THE DYNAMICS OF THE OCEAN SURFACE

by Willard Bascom

ILLUSTRATIONS BY THE AUTHOR

Published by Anchor Books
Doubleday & Company, Inc.
Garden City, New York

FOR ANITRA

THE SCIENCE STUDY SERIES

The Science Study Series offers to students and to the general public the writing of distinguished authors on the most stirring and fundamental topics of science, from the smallest known particles to the whole universe. Some of the books tell of the role of science in the world of man, his technology and civilization. Others are biographical in nature, telling the fascinating stories of the great discoverers and their discoveries. All the authors have been selected both for expertness in the fields they discuss and for ability to communicate their special knowledge and their own views in an interesting way. The primary purpose of these books is to provide a survey within the grasp of the young student or the layman. Many of the books, it is hoped, will encourage the reader to make his own investigations of natural phenomena.

The Series, which now offers topics in all the sciences and their applications, had its beginning in a project to revise the secondary schools' physics curriculum. At the Massachusetts Institute of Technology during 1956 a group of physicists, high school teachers, journalists, apparatus designers, film producers, and other specialists organized the Physical Science Study Committee, now operating as a part of Educational Services Incorporated, Watertown, Massachusetts. They pooled their knowledge and experience toward the design and creation of aids to the learning of physics. Initially their effort was supported by the National Science Foundation, which has continued to aid the program. The Ford Foundation, the Fund for the Advancement of Education, and the Alfred P. Sloan Foundation have also given support. The Committee has created a textbook, an extensive film series, a laboratory guide, especially designed apparatus, and a teacher's source book.

The Series is guided by a Board of Editors, consisting of Bruce F. Kingsbury, Managing Editor; John H. Durston, General Editor; Paul F. Brandwein, the Conservation Foundation and Harcourt, Brace & World, Inc.; Samuel A. Goudsmit, Brookhaven National Laboratory; Philippe LeCorbeiller, Harvard University, and Gerard Piel, *Scientific American*.

CONTENTS

THE SCIENCE STUDY SERIES   ix

PROLOGUE   1

I. INTRODUCTION   3

The Earth and Its Waters. The Wave
Spectrum. The Edge of the Land. Beaches
as Major Coastal Features.

II. IDEAL WAVES   24

The First Wave Theory. The Wave Channel. The Fundamental Properties of
Waves. Orbital Motion. Mass Transport.

III. WIND WAVES   42

Sea Waves. Great Storm Waves. Oil on
Troubled Waters. Swell.

IV. WAVES IN SHALLOW WATER   66

Reflection. Diffraction. Refraction. Storm
Surges.

V. TIDES AND SEICHES   82

The Tides. Tidal Bores. Seiching.

VI. IMPULSIVELY GENERATED WAVES   102

Seismic Sea Waves. Tsunami Warning

Systems. Explosion-Generated Waves.
Waves Produced by Ships. Surfing on
Waves.

VII. MEASURING WAVES AND MAKING WAVES   130

Wave Observations. Tide Gauges. Wave
Recorders. Wave Force Measurement.
Making Waves.

VIII. THE SURF   158

Breaking Waves. Surf Beat. Undertow
and Rip Currents. Surveying in the Surf.

IX. BEACHES   184

Beach Materials. Sand Motion. Berms
and Bars. Minor Beach Features.

X. THE LITTORAL CONVEYOR BELT   213

Shoreline Erosion. The Longshore Transport of Sand. What to Do about Littoral
Drift. The Effect of Groins.

XI. MAN AGAINST THE SEA   236

Waves Attack. Man Defends. The Design
of Shoreline Structures.

EPILOGUE   257

ADDITIONAL READING   259

INDEX   261

PROLOGUE

Is there anyone who can watch without fascination the struggle for supremacy between sea and land?

The sea attacks relentlessly, marshaling the force of its powerful waves against the land's strongest points. It collects the energy of distant winds and transports it across thousands of miles of open ocean as quietly rolling swell. On nearing shore this calm disguise is suddenly cast off, and the waves rise up in angry breakers, hurling themselves against the land in final furious assault. Turbulent water, green and white, is flung against the sea cliffs and forced in the cracks between the rocks to dislodge them. When the pieces fall, the churning water grinds them against each other to form sand; the sand already on the beach melts away before the onslaught.

But the land defends itself with such subtle skill that often it will gain ground in the face of the attack. Sometimes it will trade a narrow zone of high cliff for a wide low beach. Or it may use some of its beach material in a flanking maneuver to seal off arms of the sea that have recklessly reached between headlands. The land constantly straightens its front to present the least possible shoreline to the sea's onslaught.

1

When the great storm waves come, the beach will temporarily retreat, slyly deploying part of its material in a sandy underwater bar that forces the waves to break prematurely and spend their energies in futile foam and turbulence before they reach the main coast. When the storm subsides, the small waves that follow contritely return the sand to widen the beach again. Rarely can either of the antagonists claim a permanent victory.

This shifting battleground is the surf zone. The two combatants—waves and beaches—are the heroes of this book.

Chapter I

INTRODUCTION

Waves are undulating forms that move along the surface of the sea. They may exist on the interface between any two fluids of different density, but this book will deal only with those that travel on the surface between ocean and atmosphere. While any kind of disturbance in the water is likely to generate waves, there are three prime natural causes: wind, earthquakes, and the gravitational pull of the moon and the sun.

Wind waves are the most familiar kind; they are also the most variable and in many ways the most puzzling. The size and variety of the waves raised by the wind depend on three factors: the velocity of the wind, the distance it blows across the water, the length of time it blows. Moreover, the character of the waves changes markedly as they move away from the winds that created them.

The earthquake mechanism is simpler. A rapid motion of the subsea rocks disturbs a mass of water. In regaining its equilibrium the water surface oscillates up and down and sends out a series of seismic sea waves, collectively called a *tsunami*.

The tides, which are a special kind of very long waves, are caused by the earth's turning beneath

3

great bulges of water raised by the combined gravitational fields of the moon and the sun.

However generated, the character of waves and the velocity at which they move are influenced by the depth of the water in which they are traveling. Therefore, in order to understand the behavior of waves, one must also know something about the shapes of the rocky basins that hold the water. Consider the beginnings of the water and the land—the origin of the earth's surface features.

THE EARTH AND ITS WATERS

The earth formed from rocky and metallic fragments left over from the construction of the sun—debris that was swept up by a rocky nucleus and attracted together into a single body by the force of gravity. The original materials were cold as outer space and dry as dust; whatever water and gases they contained were locked inside individual fragments as chemical compounds. The impact of the collisions as the fragments joined, plus the enormous internal pressure caused by gravity, caused the new earth to heat up. It may never have been any hotter than it is now, but the internal temperature was such that the compounds broke down, releasing the water and gases. Plastic flow could occur. Segregation by density began, and earth started to organize into its present layered structure. The heaviest metals sank to the center; the lightest materials migrated outward.

In time the lightest rocks—granites—reached the surface and collected into the large blocks now known as continents. Between them were broad low-

4

lands, which became the ocean basins. At the same time water and gases were brought to the surface by volcanic activity. Slowly the ocean basins filled and an atmosphere formed. In a few billion years the ocean was full and the atmosphere was sufficiently dense that effective winds could exist to transport water vapor. As soon as the evaporation-condensa-

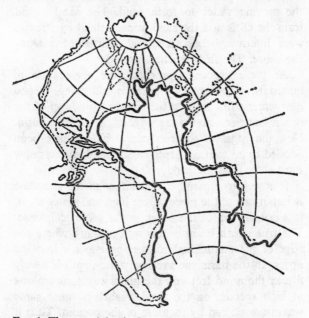

Fig. 1. The true Atlantic Ocean basin is not bounded by its shoreline.

tion cycle could operate, rains fell and stream erosion began. Fragments of continental rock were carried downhill by the running water and deposited in the ocean. The coarser particles were deposited close to shore; the finer ones were carried out to deep water, where they formed sedimentary deposits that tended to smooth the sea floor and raise the sea level. The motions of the new atmosphere created the first waves and these waves began the attack on the primordial shorelines. Then as now the waves undermined sea cliffs, bringing down large chunks of rock, which were patiently ground against each other by the moving water to form sand. The sand mined from the cliffs and the sand mined inland by streams were intermingled, sorted, and redistributed along the shore. The first beaches formed.

As these processes proceed (the segregation of materials in the earth's interior is still going on and new water still comes to the surface) the level of the ocean has risen above the edge of its natural basin. Now the edges of the continental blocks have been flooded to an average depth of six hundred feet; now most shorelines are sandy.

It is well to remember that although the shoreline is important as the place where land and water meet, it is not the rim of the ocean in the geological sense. The true ocean basin begins well offshore where the edge of the continental rock slopes steeply into the abyss. In the basin the average water depth is nearly fifteen thousand feet and the great waves race along at high speeds; on the shallow shelves these same waves are slowed by the drag of the bottom. Thus it is on the shallow continental shelves that many of the phenomena described in this book occur. There, waves moving landward from the deep ocean are transformed as they first feel the bottom; there, beaches are created and constantly rearranged; there, man's shoreline works must meet and resist the force of the ocean's waves.

Waves come in many kinds and sizes; it is best to think of them as a continuous spectrum extending from waves so small they can hardly be seen to waves so long they are not noticed. Somewhere in the midst of the spectrum are the waves with which we are all familiar.

THE WAVE SPECTRUM

Waves range in size from the ripples in a pond to the great storm waves of the ocean and the tides whose wave length is half the distance around the

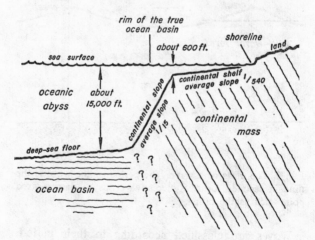

FIG. 2. The contact between ocean and continent.

earth. In order to be able to discuss such widely varying kinds and sizes of waves it is necessary to agree on a standard set of names for the parts of a wave.

The principal ones are defined as follows:

Crest: The high point of a wave
Trough: The low point of a wave
Wave height: Vertical distance from trough to crest
Wave length: Horizontal distance between adjacent crests
Wave period: The time in seconds for a wave crest to trav-
                erse a distance equal to one wave length

(There is a direct relationship between wave period and wave length, but wave height is independent of either.)

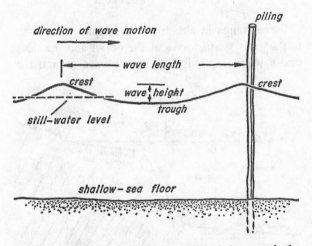

FIG. 3. The parts of a wave. The period of the wave is the time in seconds for two successive crests to pass a fixed point such as the piling.

Waves are classified according to their period, which ranges from less than one second to more than ten thousand seconds. The energy spectrum diagram prepared by Professor Walter Munk of the Scripps Institution of Oceanography shows that the energy in the ocean is distributed among several major groups of waves, each with a characteristic range of periods.

Beginning at the lower end of the spectrum with the very-short-period waves, we have in order: ripples, with periods of fractional seconds; wind chop of one to four seconds; fully developed seas, five to twelve seconds; swell, six to sixteen seconds, surf beat of about one to three minutes, tsunamis of ten to twenty minutes, and tides with periods of twelve or twenty-four hours. Thus there are many kinds of waves, each generated and developed in a special way.

The simultaneous existence of so many kinds and sizes of waves on the surface of the ocean, coming from different sources, moving in many directions,

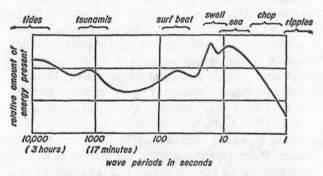

FIG. 4. The ocean wave spectrum. (after Walter Munk)

and changing inexplicably from day to day made it difficult for man to learn the ways of waves.

Toss a pebble in a puddle. The impulse generates a series of similar waves, which move outward in all directions. The simple circular pattern is clear until the first waves reach shore and are reflected backward. Now the pattern is not so simple, for the wave fronts of the returning waves interfere with the outgoing waves. The two sets of waves form curious patterns with diamond-shaped high points where crests coincide. As the reflections from the other sides of the puddle are added, the interference pattern becomes very complex. For a few moments there is hopeless jumble of high points moving in all directions; then the whole surface flattens back to mirror-like calm. You could perform that seemingly simple experiment a hundred times and still not clearly understand what happened.

In the ocean the situation is far more complicated. First, the source of the waves is rarely an impulse at a point—usually it is gusty wind blowing over a broad area that creates very irregular wave shapes. Second, waves change in character as they leave the generating area and travel long distances. Third, usually several sets of waves with different periods and directions are present at the same time. Fourth, waves are greatly influenced by the undersea topography. When they approach shore and move into shallow water, the wave fronts bend and the waves break, expending their energy in foam and turbulence. Plainly, questions about the manner in which waves are born, develop, travel, and die could not be answered by casual observers.

Ocean waves are so hopelessly complex that thousands of years of observations produced only the obvious explanation that somehow waves are raised by the wind. The higher the wind, the bigger the waves, of course.

The description of the sea surface remained in

the province of the poet, who found it ". . . troubled, unsettled, restless. Purring with ripples under the caress of a breeze, flying into scattered billows before the torment of a storm and flung as raging surf against the land; heaving with tides breathed by the sleeping giant beneath." A fanciful but quite useless description of the wave spectrum.

Now after over a hundred years of scientific work, including a concentrated effort for the last twenty years, most of the major features of waves and their causes can be satisfactorily explained in mathematical terms and reproduced experimentally. In fact, the theoreticians have become so bold as a result of the success of their complicated equations that there is danger the study of waves will fall entirely into the hands of men who have never seen the sea. In this book the descriptive wave researchers will make a determined last stand, and the mathematical description will be held to a minimum.

The Edge of the Land

The crust of the earth is slowly but constantly shifting. The continents act much like great rafts of rock, floating on the viscous interior of the earth. Consequently, if a load is added to the top of the raft—by a huge volcanic outpouring of lava or the accumulation of a great mass of ice—the raft will sink and sea level will appear to rise. By the same reasoning, as erosion removes mountains and large ice sheets melt, the load is lightened and the land rises. To illustrate, a number of embayments on the Alaska coast that were used as harbors a century

11

ago are now too shallow to be navigable because that part of the continent has risen. Other forces deep in the earth also cause the great blocks of continental rock to move up and down and the ocean level to rise and fall. These major crustal movements occur very slowly, but as they do, the shoreline, which is especially sensitive to such changes, advances and retreats.

Many geologists classify coasts according to whether they are submerging or emerging from the sea and whether erosion of rock or deposition of sediment has the upper hand. For example, much of the central California coast, from Monterey to Mendocino, is rising. This movement is evidenced by the existence of terrace-like remnants of old sea bottom now well above the sea. Along our northwest coast (Puget Sound) and northeast coast (Hudson River Valley to Maine), large segments are described as "drowned topography," meaning that the land has sunk relative to sea level. Since the original topography was largely hills and valleys, in both these areas the shoreline is very irregular. Beaches tend to be narrow, short, and rocky; they do not form an important part of the coast.

Most of the rest of the east coast from New Jersey to Florida is nearly straight because the submerged land has a long gentle slope that extends from many miles inland to the edge of the continental shelf, a hundred miles offshore. This coast is stable, not having changed its elevation with respect to the ocean for a long period of time. It is characterized by an almost continuous line of sandy barrier islands with great wide beaches. Between these elongated islands and the mainland are a series of shallow bays and lagoons. Thus the basic geology of a coast depends

12

on its history of motion relative to the ocean. If there is an ample sand supply and if enough time elapses without a major change in elevation, the beach will become an influential part of the coast.

Most coasts have a rather complicated geologic history. Relative to sea level they have at various times emerged and submerged again, each time retaining some features left from the previous situation. Moreover, since the marine processes are usually interrupted before they are complete, there

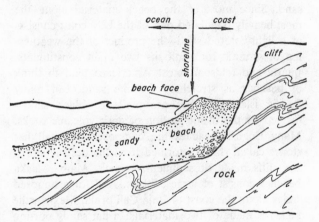

FIG. 5. Coast, shoreline, and beach.

are relatively few examples of finished work. The geologist is thus forced to observe changing situations and guess how the process started and what forms it will eventually produce. His principal concern is to determine the mechanism that causes the changes and the rate at which the changes are taking place. Then, perhaps, he can forecast the future.

Let us start by clearing up three terms that may cause some confusion. A shoreline is the line of contact between water and land. A coast is a large physiographic feature often extending several miles inland from the shore and several hundred miles along it. By comparison a beach is a relatively small feature whose limits are defined by the effects of waves.

A beach is an accumulation of rock fragments subject to movement by ordinary wave action. Beaches may be composed of any kind or color of rocky material, ranging in size from boulders to fine sand. Since most of the beach material along the most heavily populated part of the U.S. coast consists of a light-colored sand—the product of the weathering of granitic rock into its two main constituents, quartz and feldspar—most Americans tend to think of beaches as stretches of white sand. But many Pacific island beaches are made of black sand—formed by the disintegration of dark volcanic rocks. Many English beaches are composed of small flat stones called shingle, formed from the destruction of sea cliffs made of sedimentary rock. Many Alaska beaches consist of large cobbles. And for a hundred miles along the coast of Baja California, Mexico, the beach is made of two materials: a flat sandy portion that is exposed only at low tide, while immediately above and behind the sand, great cobble ramparts rise to a height of thirty feet or more. So, one's idea of a beach depends on one's experience. In this book, for convenience, all beach material will be called sand, although it is recognized that all of the features described may be formed in pebbles or shingle or cobbles.

There are two ways to think about beaches: (1) as small closed systems in which the sand moves either on-and-off shore at the whim of the waves, or alongshore in accordance with currents; (2) as geologic units of considerable size.

BEACHES AS MAJOR COASTAL FEATURES

Later in this book the first of these beach processes will be discussed in some detail, but in considering the mechanisms by which beaches shift with the waves one tends to think on a small scale and to lose sight of the fact that beaches are often of grand enough scale to be worthy of study as major coastal features. Although the comprehensive consideration of beaches in this physiographic sense is beyond the scope of this book, let us at least briefly consider the three forms that beaches are most likely to take when they are treated as geologic units. A beach can be simply a narrow strip of sand separating the rocky cliffs of land from the sea; a spit or a bay-mouth bar; a barrier island.

The first form—beaches that are narrow, of limited extent, and on which the sand is a shallow veneer over the rock—is indicative of a youthful shoreline. That is, not much time has passed, geologically speaking, since the last change in sea level. What little sand there is has been created in place by the undermining of the cliff and the grinding of the rocks by wave action. Many beaches of the California-Oregon coast are in this category. These so-called pocket beaches extend between rocky headlands and often have sheer cliffs behind; in the winter months storms strip off most of the sand, exposing cobbles and the underlying rocks.

15

The second form, in which spits and bay-mouth bars are created by wave action, requires more time to develop. In it, rough coasts tend to be straightened by wave forces and ragged shorelines smoothed. Headlands extending into the sea are attacked because wave energy is focused on them by the underwater topography. Waves striking the coast at an angle create alongshore currents which transport sand and seal off the mouths of relatively quiet bays.

The sequence of events in one form of coastal straightening is illustrated in Figure 6. At stage one, bold headlands project into ocean where they are attacked by waves whose energy is concentrated there by the process of wave refraction. As the headland retreats and the cliffs are reduced to rocky fragments, currents caused by the waves striking the shore obliquely transport the smaller particles into the relatively quiet water at the head of the bay where they form a beach (stage two). Later, the headlands cut back and the bay becomes shallow as in stage three. The longshore coastal currents, which were disorganized by turbulence around the headlands in the earlier stages, now become dominant and sweep sand along the coast creating bay-mouth beaches. With a straight shoreline, sand can be transported considerable distances, passing headlands and bays alike in its longshore migration. Eventually at the land's end, the water deepens and the transporting current spreads out and is reduced in velocity so that the sand it has been carrying drops to the bottom. These embankment-like deposits in which the outermost end is surrounded by water are called spits. They form wherever there is a supply of sand, a transporting current, and a dumping ground.

There are two famous spits at the entrance to New York harbor. Sandy Hook, to the south, was built by materials supplied by the erosion and retreat of the Navesink highlands. It grew steadily until it

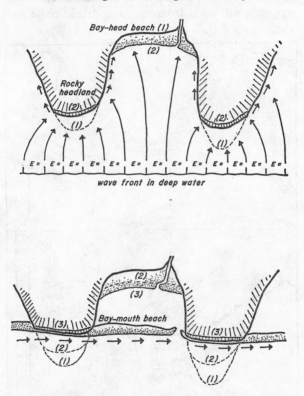

FIG. 6. Waves straighten a rocky coast. *Top:* Zones of equal wave energy in deep water are concentrated by wave refraction so that headlands are attacked. *Bottom:* Eventually headlands are cut back and furnish enough sand to build a straight continuous beach.

reached an equilibrium situation in which the new sand added to the tip is just equal to that removed by the tidal currents at the harbor mouth.

Rockaway spit, northeast of the harbor entrance, was built with sand from the Long Island coast and

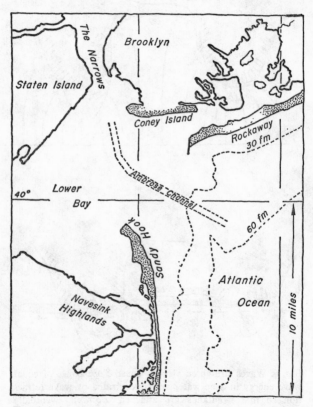

FIG. 7. Spits at New York harbor entrance (Sandy Hook and Rockaway).

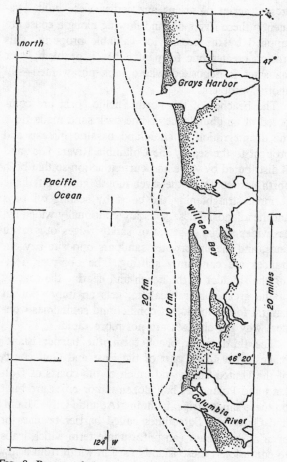

FIG. 8. Bay-mouth bars on the Washington coast near the Columbia River entrance.

grew at the rate of two hundred feet a year (one mile in twenty-three years) for a long period until the present series of groins and jetties were built. Frequently these rivers of sand flowing along a coast are supplied by the erosion of valuable property. This erosion creates one form of a beach problem; later the sand is deposited where it is not wanted—still another problem.

The beaches of the north Pacific coast are composed of an abundance of fine dark sand made from the disintegration of an inland basaltic plateau and brought to the sea by the Columbia River. The sand is distributed by wave and current action so that both north and south of the river mouth great spits have formed, straightening the coast by sealing off bays and headlands. These spits are continually widening, as evidenced by a series of sandy ridges or growth lines, and the underwater sandbars opposite bay entrances are constantly shifting. The observer, feeling the shudder of the beach and hearing the roaring of the great winter breakers, gets an impression of natural forces in violent conflict and sometimes wonders why the changes are not more rapid.

The third major beach form, the barrier island, makes up a major part of the East and Gulf coasts of the United States and much of the coasts of Holland and Poland. A half dozen major cities are built on these sandy strips, including Atlantic City, Miami, and Galveston. Sometimes called barrier beaches or even offshore bars (an unfortunate term which leads to confusion), these islands vary in width from a few yards to a mile. They may be dozens of miles long and are, in places, separated from the mainland by shallow bays many miles wide.

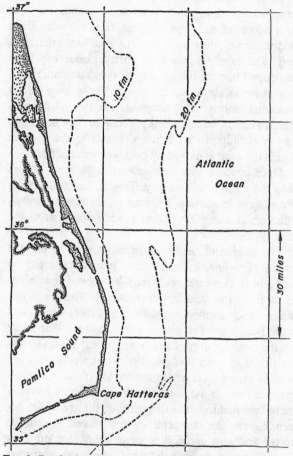

FIG. 9. Barrier beaches extend along much of the U.S. east coast. Cape Hatteras, on a long narrow ridge of sand, lies well off the main Carolina coast.

When sand is blown by the wind into dunes, as at Kitty Hawk, North Carolina, where the Wright brothers first flew, the hills on these islands may rise to a height of nearly a hundred feet. Between them and the main coast there is a chain of bays, marshes, and tidal lagoons, which in many places has been developed into an inland waterway where small craft can move safely along the coast. These large sandy shoreline forms are accumulated beach deposits which are now so large and permanent they no longer fit our definition that limits a beach to the area in which the sand is moved by ordinary wave action.

Since beaches owe their existence to wave action, they have a dynamic quality. That is, beach materials are always in motion—as long as there are waves—although this mobility is not readily apparent to the casual observer.

The motion of the beach material may be parallel to the shoreline, in which case it is transported by alongshore currents, or it may be moved toward or away from the land by wave action. There are two major beach forms created by the waves: berms and bars. Berms are flat, above-water features that make up the familiar part of the beach. Bars are underwater ridges of sand that parallel the shoreline and are seldom seen except at unusually low tides. On most beaches there is a constant exchange of sand between these two features, the direction of the transport depending on the character of the waves. When the waves are large and follow close upon each other as they do under storm conditions, the berm is eroded and the bar builds up. When calm conditions return, the small waves rebuild the berm at the expense of the bar. For this reason the above-water part of a beach is generally much narrower in the stormy winter months than in the summer. This is convenient for the hordes of bathers who come to sun themselves on the wide summer berm and swim in the low surf.

The steeply sloping seaward side of the berm against which the waves are in constant contact is the beach face. The face might also be described as the zone within which the shoreline wanders as the waves rush up the beach and wash back down it.

It is necessary to set limits on the extent of a beach to keep the discussion of its properties within reasonable bounds. In the seaward direction, beaches extend outward as far as ordinary waves move the sand particles. By experiment and repeated measurement, this limit has been found to be about thirty feet below the low-tide level. This is an arbitrary but satisfactory limit that is generally accepted. Above water, the beach extends landward to the edge of the permanent coast. The latter may consist of a cliff, sand dunes, or man-made structures. In the geological sense these are not really permanent, but they endure far longer than the small-scale beach features that concern us here.

This rather broad description of the major features of waves and beaches is intended to illuminate the subject generally so that the ideas developed in the following chapters will fit into a recognizable framework.

Chapter II

IDEAL WAVES

The shape and motion of the ocean surface as waves pass across it are very complicated. It is little wonder that even after thousands of years of observation, seafaring men developed no very satisfactory explanation of the mechanics of wave motion. Ancient mariners knew in a general way that waves were generated by the winds, that they continued to travel outside the storm area, and that on entering shallow water they would rise up and break, expending their energy on a beach or against a rocky headland. These characteristics were easily observable.

A major difficulty in explaining their origin and motion came from the fact that waves are so irregular. Shipboard observers could see that when a breeze suddenly sprang up, a previously calm sea would first become rippled, and that in time and as the wind increased, these ripples would grow into larger and larger waves. Soon the ship would be surrounded by a full-fledged storm with large irregular masses of water moving on all sides, often breaking on the deck. There was no longer any chance to observe—the problem was to survive. Out away from the generating area the waves were noticed to be somewhat more regular. But even at a distance the

24

observations were confused by the simultaneous existence of several trains of waves from different storms and by the curious effect of the underwater topography.

Observers on shore would see high waves intermixed with low ones; several would arrive in quick succession, then the time between waves would be long; some would break, others not. In the midst of a period of calm weather and blue skies, suddenly, great waves would arrive at a shore. No general set of rules for wave behavior could be worked out that seemed to cover all the conditions observed. They could only say, "That is just the nature of waves."

The obvious way to attack such a complicated problem is to deal with each of the components, one at a time, in their simplest form. The first problem was to define wave properties or dimensions and to determine the relationship between them. Then it would be necessary to discover what size and duration of storm and what velocity of wind created what kinds and sizes of waves. Finally the relationship between wave motion and the depth of water would have to be worked out.

It seems easy now, with the advantage of hindsight, to organize the wave research program that could have been carried out many years ago, but, of course, nothing so systematic happened. Casual observations of many wave characteristics gradually led, step by step, to sufficient understanding that a beginning could be made on wave theory.

One can imagine that several of the important properties of waves were first thoughtfully noted many thousands of years ago by someone living on the shore of the Mediterranean Sea. Probably this early scientist was regarded as the village loafer; probably he made his observations in a little cove with clear shallow water, a sandy bottom and an occasional stalk of seaweed. He would sit on one shore and watch the waves of the sea move into the cove.

One bright and sunny day when no breeze blew to ruffle the surface of the water, a series of regular waves entered the cove, moved across it, and broke on the beach at its head. Idly this scientist-by-accident tossed a stick into the water and watched it float there, noting its position in relation to a rock on the opposite shore. It would rise and fall, move back and forth, as waves passed under it, but it did not move shoreward with the waves. There was

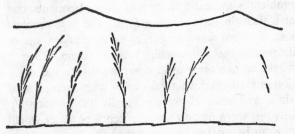

FIG. 10. Motions of seaweed indicate the movements of water particles as a wave passes.

nothing new or startling here; he, and others, had seen this countless times before. But suddenly this man saw in his mind the fact that waves are only moving forms and that the water stays in the same place. The stick, and the water around it, moved in a slow circular oscillation as each wave passed.

Now he looked more carefully at the seaweed stalks growing upright from the bottom. As a crest approached, he noticed, the upper part of the weed moved toward it; as the crest passed, the weed continued to point toward it until a new crest approached. Fragments of weed suspended in the water that were neither floating nor sinking, moved in slow vertical circles, one for each passing wave. Here was a basic principle of hydrodynamics: objects in the water tend to do what the water they displace would have done. The water particles also must be moving in circles.

With these simple observations oscillatory waves were discovered. This was an accomplishment roughly equivalent to Newton's observation that an apple falls to the ground because of the force of gravity. Everyone had seen, but no one had thought about what it meant. Unlike Newton, the early wave-observer was not capable of expressing what he had seen in mathematical terms.

The First Wave Theory

Much, much later, in 1802, Franz Gerstner, of Czechoslovakia, produced the first rather primitive wave theory. He described how water particles in a wave move in circles, and he pointed out that those in the crest of a wave move in the direction of wave advance and those in the trough move in the opposite direction. Gerstner noted that before returning to its original position each water particle at the surface traces a circular orbit, the diameter of which is exactly equal to the height of the passing wave. He observed that the surface trace of a wave is approximately a trochoid, the curve described by a point on a circle as the circle is rolled along the underside of a line. Presumably he knew that if the wave height is small compared to the length, as it is for most water waves, the shape of the trochoid approaches that of a sine curve.

Such was the theoretical beginning. Gerstner's work was found later to have several inconsistencies, but it attracted the attention of the Weber brothers,

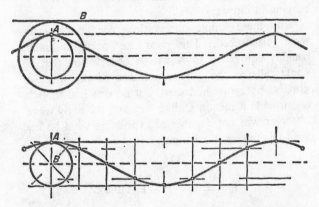

FIG. 11. Geometrical wave forms for waves of equal lengths and heights. *Top:* A trochoidal wave is generated by point *A* as outer circle rolls along the underside of line *B*. *Bottom:* A sine wave is generated by projecting the position of point *A* to equal increments of time as it rotates about a stationary center *B*.

Ernst and Wilhelm, of Germany, who became the first experimentalists. In 1825 they published a book about their findings with a wave channel. It was a glass-walled tank five feet long, a foot deep and an inch wide. They filled this tank on various occasions with brandy and mercury as well as with water. To make waves they would suck up some of the fluid with a tube and let it fall back again. Thus began the study of waves under controlled conditions. The flat-sided tank, the opportunity to study one wave at a time at eye level, and the chance to repeat an experiment over and over until understanding was achieved, overcame the major difficulties of studying waves in nature.

The Webers discovered that waves are reflected from a vertical wall without loss of energy; they watched suspended particles to confirm the theory that the circular orbits diminished in size with depth; they found that near the bottom the orbits were greatly flattened. In order to determine the shape of the water surface, a chalk-dusted slate was quickly plunged in and withdrawn.

The early theoreticians devised equations in which an endless train of perfect waves, all exactly alike, moved across an ocean of infinite breadth and depth. Their trains were an unreal abstraction, but the method was the most reasonable way to begin to work out the relationships between period and wave length and velocity for sinusoidal ocean waves. These equations were then applied to the waves observed in wave channels.

In the mid-1800s there was a great flurry of experimental work. Scott Russell, of England, built a channel about one foot square and twenty feet long. Near one end was a removable sluice gate that created a small reservoir. To make waves Russell would suddenly raise the gate and allow the water to rush down the channel as a solitary wave or wave of translation. This impulse produced normal waves, which would then reflect back and forth between the ends, sixty reflections giving him an effective channel length of twelve hundred feet. He made the first careful measurements of wave velocity. In France, Henri Bazin made similar experiments in a larger channel and obtained similar results.

The development of equations and the serious attempt to understand theoretically what the waves in tank and ocean were doing was a big step. But we must remember that with equations the experimenter has true models in his wave channel; without them he has only a plaything.

TABLE I

THE PROGRESS OF WAVE RESEARCH
AS HIGHLIGHTED BY MILESTONES IN THE LITERATURE

1802   Franz V. Gerstner, "Theory of Waves," Czechoslovakia.

1825   Ernst Weber and Wilhelm Weber, "Experimental Studies of Waves," Austria.

1837   J. Scott Russell, "Report on Waves," British Association for the Advancement of Science.

1845   Sir George Airy, "On Tides and Waves," Encyclopedia Metropolitan, England.

1863   W. J. M. Rankine, "On the Exact Form of Waves Near the Surface of Deep Water," Royal Society of London.

1864   Thomas Stevenson, "The Construction of Harbors," England.

1877   Lord Rayleigh, "On Progressive Waves," London Mathematical Society.

1880   George G. Stokes, "On the Theory of Oscillatory Waves," England.

1904   D. D. Gaillard, "Wave Action in Relation to Engineering Structures," U. S. Army Engineers.

1911   Vaughan Cornish, "Waves of the Sea and Other Water Waves," England.

1925 Sir Harold Jeffries, "On the Formation of Water Waves by the Wind," England.

1931 H. Thorade, "Probleme der Wasserwellen," Germany.

1932 Horace Lamb, "Hydrodynamics," England.

1942 Morrough P. O'Brien, "A Summary of the Theory of Oscillatory Waves," Beach Erosion Board, U.S.A.

1947 H. U. Sverdrup and W. H. Munk, "Wind, Sea and Swell," Hydrographic Office, USN.

1955 W. J. Pierson, G. Neumann, and R. W. James, "Practical Methods for Observing and Forecasting Ocean Waves by Means of Wave Spectra and Statistics," U.S.A.

1963 "Ocean Wave Spectra," USN Oceanographic Office and U. S. National Research Council Symposium.

The theoretical and experimental work done today is more complicated because it is now realized that ocean waves are not really sinusoidal, or any other pure mathematical shape. Now real ocean waves are dealt with statistically as combinations of great numbers of small waves. Model work today is done for the same reason that it was done long ago—to simplify the problems by working under controlled conditions. The Mediterranean cove has been replaced by the experimental wave channel and the irregular swell by precision generators.

Today dozens of fluid mechanics laboratories have facilities for modeling waves and determining their effects on beaches and ships. These facilities range from the tabletop ripple-makers to huge tanks that can create breakers eight feet high on full-size dam models. Let us begin this research into the nature of waves by experimenting in the simple form of wave channel shown in Figure 12.

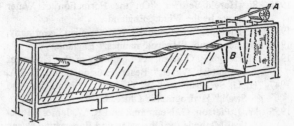

Fig. 12. Glass-sided wave channel. A variable-speed motor with an adjustable yoke drives a paddle, hinged at the bottom, to generate waves with periods of 0.7 to 1.4 seconds and heights up to one foot. The waves on the backside of the generator are absorbed by special screens.

THE WAVE CHANNEL

The first problem of the researcher is to generate an endless train of ideal waves so that their properties can be studied. The simplest form of waves to generate and the easiest to understand mathematically is the sine.

The main features of a wave channel are evident in the illustration. It is simply a glass-sided tank that permits the researcher to look inside a wave. At one end is a movable paddle which fits closely but can slide against the walls of the tank; it is hinged at the bottom and driven at the top by a connecting rod, which, in turn, is attached to an arm on a variable-speed electric motor. The point of attachment of the rod to the motor arm is adjustable so that the height of the waves can be varied. (The farther out on the arm, the bigger the waves.) The period of the model waves is adjusted by changing the speed of the motor. At the other end of the tank the waves break on a beach, which may merely absorb the waves, and prevent confusing reflections, or be part of the experiment. The moving paddle also generates waves on its back side, and it is customary to fill this space with some material, such as synthetic honeycomb, that immediately dissipates these unwanted waves in local turbulence. Finally, a checkerboard of squares is marked on the glass walls so that wave height and length can be read directly.

The Fundamental Properties of Waves

Now we are equipped to learn the fundamental properties of waves. In the usual fashion of experimenters, our plan is to vary one thing at a time, keeping all others constant and measuring the changes produced. First, the motor is run at one revolution per second; then its speed is increased in a series of steps while the water depth and the arm setting stay the same. Changing motor speed is equivalent to changing the period—the time for the flap to complete one cycle. This control also changes the wave length, as one would expect. However, we notice that wave height is not affected because the amount of motion of the flap is the same. Wave length depends upon period; wave height does not.

In the ideal conditions of this channel, the first experimental data confirm that pure sine waves are being produced. We rediscover that the wave length L, is equal to 5.12 times the square of the period.

$$L = \frac{g}{2\pi} T^2 \text{ or } 5.12 \ T^2$$

where g is the acceleration of gravity (32 ft/sec/sec) and T is period in seconds. Thus a one-second wave would be 5.12 feet long. Wave velocity is usually designated by C, and $C = \sqrt{\dfrac{gL}{2\pi}}$. A one-second wave in the tank verifies the relationship by moving at 5.1 feet per second.

But, as the period is increased, one soon finds that these relationships for length and velocity do not hold exactly in this wave tank for periods of over one second. Why? Because in the shorter period range we have been dealing with "deep-water waves." A "shallow-water wave" is one that is traveling in water whose depth is less than half the wave length; that is, if the depth of water is small compared to the wave length, the effect of the bottom is sufficient to alter substantially the character of the waves. With the still-water depth in our tank at 2.5 feet, increasing the period has produced waves which "feel the bottom" and are affected by it. In the full expression for wave velocity, water depth (d) is taken into account:

$$C = \sqrt{\frac{gL}{2\pi} \tan h \frac{2\pi d}{L}}$$

The final term contains the ratio $\dfrac{d}{L}$ or $\dfrac{\text{water depth}}{\text{wave length}}$. Most wave researchers find it convenient to describe waves in terms of their d/L and use a simplified version of that equation. For a d/L of more than 0.5 (a deep-water wave) the hyperbolic tangent of $\dfrac{2\pi d}{L}$ is so close to one it can be neglected, as we did earlier. On the other hand, if the depth is quite small compared to the wave length $(d/L = 0.05)$ the

$\tan h \dfrac{2\pi d}{L}$ can be replaced by simply $\dfrac{2\pi d}{L}$. Then, after cancellation, the wave-velocity expression becomes merely:

$$C = \sqrt{gd}$$

This, too, is very convenient, especially when one is working with seismic sea waves which are so long that for them even the deepest ocean is shallow water. But for values of d/L between 0.05 and 0.5 we must use the longer form of the equation. If the length-velocity equations get too sticky one can always get a copy of "Functions of d/L" compiled by Robert Wiegel of the University of California fluid mechanics laboratory and look up the answers.

We first observed that the wave height seemed to be independent of both the period and wave length, but further experiments show this is not quite so. If we hold the period constant at one second (with the wave length remaining 5.12 feet) and gradually increase the wave height, we discover that waves higher than eight inches (0.75 feet) have unstable crests. That is, they tend to break as they travel down the tank. On repeating the experiment with other heights and lengths we discover that the angle at a wave crest may not be smaller than 120° or the wave will break. Stated in another way, the wave height may not be greater than one-seventh of the wave length.

This relationship of height to length (H/L) is called wave steepness.

In reviewing the notes on these last experiments we find that as the waves became steeper they also increased slightly in velocity until at 1:7, the maximum, they moved perhaps ten percent faster than the theoretical speed. However, since ocean waves rarely achieve such steepness—only in violent storms—it is customary to neglect this increase.

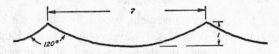

FIG. 13. Maximum wave steepness is 1:7.

When the waves move onto the abruptly shoaling beach at the end of the tank they change character in another way. As the depth decreases the waves are said to peak up; that is, their height increases rapidly. At the same time the shallow water causes the wave length to decrease, and the result is a suddenly steepened wave. In a very short distance the crest angle decreases below the critical 120° and the wave becomes unstable. The crest, moving more rapidly than the water below, falls forward and the wave form collapses into turbulent confusion, which uses up most of the wave's energy.

ORBITAL MOTION

Until now we have considered only the movement of the wave form along the surface. Now it is time to look inside the wave at the motion of the individual water particles. What do they do as a wave passes?

Since the water particles themselves cannot be seen, it is necessary to add a number of small markers to the water—they will do whatever the water does. The markers should be liquid, the same density as the water, and easily visible. One material commonly used by wave researchers is a light oil (xylol and butyl phthalate) whitened and weighted with zinc oxide. The mixture is commonly known as "gunk." By trial and error it can be mixed to almost exactly the same density as the water, and when the experiment is otherwise ready, droplets of gunk are inserted in the channel at several depths by means of a long glass tube topped by a bulb. The white globules rise or sink so slowly that they act the same as water and the results are not affected.

Now when waves are generated it is possible to see the orbital motion of these water-like particles and

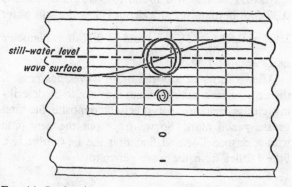

FIG. 14. Section of a wave channel with tracings on glass opposite orbiting water particles showing the change in orbit size and shape with depth.

actually to trace it out in grease pencil on the glass side of the channel. The Webers used approximately this method one hundred and fifty years ago. The solid lines in Figure 14 show the appearance of the side of the channel after the orbits of four particles of gunk at different depths have been traced out. All the orbits of particles in a vertical line describe circles in the same direction at the same time; they are in phase.

The surface particle described a circular orbit exactly equal to the height of the wave. The next one down made a somewhat smaller circle. The third orbit is not only smaller but is slightly flattened, and the one at the bottom moves back and forth in a straight line. By combining a series of such measurements with theoretical work, it has been established that at a depth of $\frac{1}{9}$ the wave length, the diameter of the orbit is approximately halved. Thus a one-second wave 0.75 foot high is found to have particle orbits 0.37 foot in diameter at a depth below the still water level of 0.57 foot $\left(\frac{5.12}{9}\right)$ and of 0.18 foot diameter at a depth of 1.14 feet.

After a series of a dozen or so waves has passed, the near-surface gunk particles are seen to be describing circles that are not precisely opposite the first grease pencil mark. So we trace out the new path with a dashed line and find that the new orbit is a little farther from the wave generator.

MASS TRANSPORT

This difference is the result of a phenomenon called mass transport. Until now we had supposed that the water returned to its original position after each wave passed, but now we find that when waves are steep the orbital circles of the water particles do not exactly close. The water itself is transported by the passing wave form, although its progress is very slow compared to the wave velocity. The volume of water so moved is negligible for waves of small steepness (the usual circumstances) and can be disregarded for all practical purposes.

However, the existence of this mass transport is a serious matter to the theoreticians. The early workers, including Gerstner and W. J. H. Rankine, concerned themselves only with "rotational flow," in which each particle completed a perfect circle as the wave form passed. Later, Sir George Airy and G. G. Stokes developed the "irrotational theory," which requires that the water move forward slightly as the wave form passes. This actual motion of the water is proportional to the square of the height of the waves and is much more pronounced at the surface than a short distance down. In a wave channel there is an imperceptibly small return flow of water along the bottom in the opposite direction to compensate for the surface transport by the waves.

One final experiment remains to be performed. We must now examine what happens to the water particles as the wave is transformed into a breaker by the sloping beach at the end of the tank. The breaking motion is too rapid to permit a particle's path to be traced in crayon on the side of the tank. Moreover, each breaker tends to disintegrate the droplets of gunk and throw them up on the beach. A more sophisticated method of recording the motion is now required. This technique uses a fast movie camera, with proper lighting, and demands a good sense of timing on the part of the men who will add the gunk and start the cameras.

With the equipment set up and a series of one-second waves rolling down the channel, one man must dip his gunk-dropper into a just-broken wave and make a trail of visible droplets while the other starts the camera. These droplets trace out the water motions inside the next breaking wave. After about a dozen tries with variations of camera speed (64 to 500 frames a second) it is reasonable to assume that the desired motion may have been captured on film at least once. Later, after processing, the pictures must be projected one frame at a time on a sheet of paper so that the successive positions of the marker drops can be plotted. When the change in positions of a series of drops is marked on the grid, along with the trace of the water surface, the result is a chart of the water motion in a breaking wave. For the same number of pictures the length of each line is directly proportional to the velocity of the water particle.

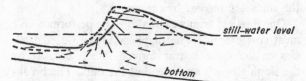

Fig. 15. Movement of water particles as a wave breaks in wave channel (from motion picture analysis).

There are many other experiments that can be made in wave tanks and we shall consider some of them in a later chapter. But now, full of confidence that we understand waves both in theory and by actual test, we fling open the laboratory door, stride to the edge of the cliff and look to sea.

Good grief! The real waves look and act nothing

like the neat ones that endlessly roll down the wave channel or march across the blackboard in orderly equations. These waves are disheveled, irregular, and moving in many directions. No alignment can be seen between a series of crests; some of the crests actually turn into troughs while we are watching them.

Should we slink back inside to our reliable equations and brood over the inconsistencies of nature? Never! Instead we must become outdoor wave researchers. It means being wet, salty, cold—and confused.

Chapter III

WIND WAVES

There are many kinds of waves in the ocean. They differ greatly in form, velocity, and origin. There are waves too long and low to see and waves that travel on density interfaces below the sea surface. Waves may be raised by ships, or landslides, or the passage of the moon, or earthquakes, or changes in atmospheric pressure. Probably there are kinds of waves that have not yet been discovered. But most waves, and the waves which are most important to mankind, are those raised by the wind.

Let us begin the life story of a wave with a perfectly smooth water surface such as a mirror-like pond. Suddenly a breeze begins to blow. Waves are born as the air pressure on the surface changes and the frictional drag of the moving air against the water creates ripples. Once a ripple has formed, there is a steep side against which the wind can press directly. Now the energy can be transferred from air to water more effectively and the small waves grow rapidly. In the ocean the same thing happens, but with no nearby shore to limit wave development the waves soon develop into a sea.

Of course, it would be rare indeed for a constant wind to blow on an entirely undisturbed ocean surface. Usually there are "old seas"—waves generated earlier by winds elsewhere. If the new wind and these existing waves are moving in about the same direction, the old waves are rapidly enlarged. If the two are opposed, the wind will flatten the sea surface as the new waves cancel the old. For the moment let us ignore this complexity.

Because winds are by nature turbulent and gusty, there are local variations in the air velocity and the pressure on the surface. As a result, wavelets of all sizes are created simultaneously.

As the waves continue to grow, the surface confronting the wind becomes higher and steeper and the process of wave building becomes more efficient —up to a point, that is, for there is a limit on how steep a wave can be. Steepness is the ratio of the height of a wave to its length, and the limit is about 1:7. A wave seven feet long can be no more than one foot high. When small steep waves exceed this limit they break, forming whitecaps. A sea surface covered with such waves is said to be choppy. When the wind blows the top off a wave, causing a breaking wave at sea, some of the energy goes into turbulence but most is contributed to longer, more stable waves. The result is that a long wave can accept more energy and rise higher than a shorter wave passing under the same wind. Therefore, as the sea surface takes energy from the wind, the small waves give way to larger ones, which can store the energy better. But new ripples and small waves are continually being formed on the slopes of the existing larger waves. Thus in the zone where the wind is moving faster than the waves, there is a wide spectrum of wave lengths. At the same time, however, the longest waves continue to accumulate energy from the smaller waves. Although the wind produces waves of many lengths, the shortest ones reach maximum height quickly and are destroyed while the longer ones continue to grow.

Three factors influence the size of wind waves. These are (1) the wind velocity, (2) the duration of the time the wind blows, (3) the extent of the open water across which it blows (the fetch). A simplified idea of the development of waves in the generating area is given in Figure 16. In this generating area

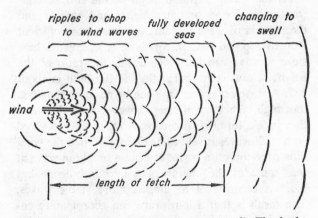

FIG. 16. The development of waves (conceptual). The fetch, within the dashed line, is the area of water on which a wind blows to generate waves. (after Richard Silvester)

(often a storm) wind waves are called sea. At the upwind end of the fetch the waves are small, but with distance they develop—their period and height increase and eventually they reach the maximum dimensions possible for the wind that is raising them.

Then the sea is said to be fully developed; that is, the waves have absorbed as much energy as they can from wind of that velocity. An extension of the fetch or a lengthening of the time would not produce larger waves.

The modern description of how the wind transfers its energy to the waves derives from the work of Harald Sverdrup and Walter Munk of the Scripps Institution of Oceanography. During World War II their attention was attracted to the problem of predicting the waves and surf that would exist on an enemy-held beach during amphibious landing operations. In *Wind, Sea and Swell* they gave the first reasonably quantitative description of how waves are generated, become swell, and move across the ocean to a distant shore.

Sea Waves

Waves in a sea do not have the regular and precise properties of waves generated in a wave channel. The height of the crests and the depths of the troughs are irregular. The length of each crest is short. In a sea, waves are merely individual hillocks of water with changing shapes that move independently. The limits of a wave in a sea are indefinable. Each mass of water which the eye selects as a wave has a different shape, a different speed, and a slightly different direction from the other waves in the sea. The words period, velocity, and wave length have lost the meaning they had in the orderly environment of the wave channel. Try to decide on the wave length of the waves in Plate IV. The spacing between waves is ex-

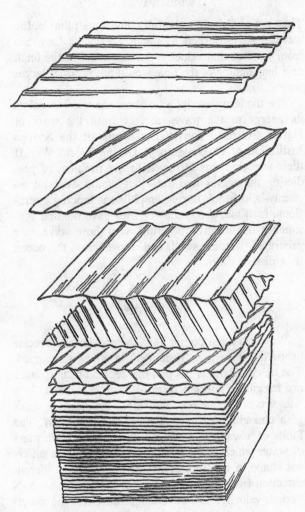

Fig. 17. The sum of many simple sine waves makes a sea. (after Willard Pierson)

ceedingly irregular and demonstrates why statistical methods must be used to describe the properties of waves in a sea. Wave heights are nearly as irregular, but fortunately waves rise from a ready reference (mean sea level) and there is somewhat less difficulty in defining wave height. For descriptive purposes, it is customary to use the average of the highest one-third of the waves (called the "significant height") and the average of the highest one-tenth of the waves. These are sometimes noted as H_3 and H_{10}.

Thus a sea is the result of superimposing a number of sinusoidal wave trains one on top of another, as shown in the accompanying conceptual diagram. Each layer represents a series of regular sine waves, as alike as those on a sheet of corrugated iron. Each layer has its own characteristic height, wave length, and direction. Individually the waves in these trains are as true to the classical formulas as those in the model tank.

The real sea surface is made up of all these layers added together. Where a number of crests coincide, there will be a high mound of water—but it will not last long, for the component waves soon go their own way. Similarly a coincidence of troughs creates an unusually low spot, also of short duration.

Since there are small wave crests in the large troughs and small depressions in the tops of the high mounds, on the average the troughs and crests of the many layers of waves tend to cancel themselves out. The more layers of waves, the more random the sea surface and the lower the average wave height.

The need to reduce these complicated irregularities to a form that would be usable by the Navy in

47

TABLE II
WIND SCALES AND SEA DESCRIPTIONS

Beaufort scale	Seaman's description of wind	Wind velocity knots	Estimating wind velocities on sea	International scale sea description and wave heights	International code for state of sea
0	Calm	Less than 1 knot	Calm; sea like a mirror.	Calm glassy 0	0
1	Light air	1 to 3 knots	Light air; ripples—no foam crests.		
2	Light breeze	4 to 6 knots	Light breeze; small wavelets, crests have glassy appearance and do not break.	Rippled 0 to 1 foot	1
3	Gentle breeze	7 to 10 knots	Gentle breeze; large wavelets, crests begin to break. Scattered whitecaps.	Smooth 1 to 2 feet	2
4	Moderate breeze	11 to 16 knots	Moderate breeze; small waves becoming longer. Frequent whitecaps.	Slight 2 to 4 feet	3
5	Fresh breeze	17 to 21 knots	Fresh breeze; moderate waves taking a more pronounced long form; mainly whitecaps, some spray.	Moderate 4 to 8 feet	4
6	Strong breeze	22 to 27 knots	Strong breeze; large waves begin to form extensive whitecaps everywhere, some spray.	Rough 8 to 13 feet	5

No.	Name	Wind speed	Description	Sea	Wave height
7	High wind (Moderate gale)	28 to 33 knots	Moderate gale; sea heaps up and white foam from breaking waves begins to be blown in streaks along the direction of the wind.	6	Very rough 13 to 20 feet
8	Gale (Fresh gale)	34 to 40 knots	Fresh gale; moderately high waves of greater length; edges of crests break into spindrift. The foam is blown in well-marked streaks along the direction of the wind.		
9	Strong gale	41 to 47 knots	Strong gale; high waves, dense streaks of foam along the direction of the wind. Spray may affect visibility. Sea begins to roll.	7	High 20 to 30 feet
10	Whole gale	48 to 55 knots	Whole gale; very high waves. The surface of the sea takes on a white appearance. The rolling of sea becomes heavy and shocklike. Visibility affected.		
11	Storm	56 to 63 knots	Storm; exceptionally high waves. Small and medium-sized ships are lost to view long periods.	8	Very high 30 to 45 feet
12	Hurricane	64 and above	Hurricane; the air is filled with foam and spray. Sea completely white with driving spray; visibility very seriously affected.	9	Phenomenal over 45 feet

wave forecasting led Willard Pierson and G. Neumann, at New York University, to a method of describing waves by means of their energy spectra. In this scheme a value is assigned to the square of the

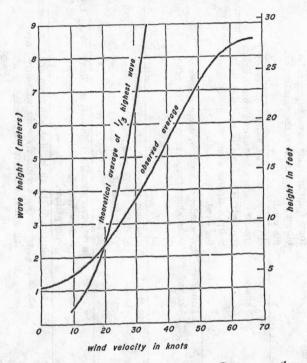

FIG. 18. Wave heights as observed by ten German weather ships in the North Atlantic (average of seventy thousand observations). (after Roll)

wave height for each frequency and direction. Then, after the portion of the spectrum where the energy is concentrated has been determined, it is possible to approximate average periods and lengths and use these in wave forecasting.

Some of the properties of wind waves are illustrated by Figure 19, in which wave period is plotted against the amount of energy contained for three wind velocities. Each curve (spectrum) represents

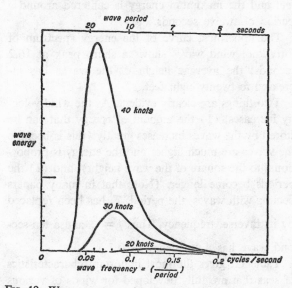

FIG. 19. Wave spectrum for fully arisen seas caused by winds of twenty, thirty, and forty knots. (after Pierson, Neumann and James)

the distribution of energy between various periods in a fully developed sea; the area under each curve represents the total energy. Consider first the twenty-knot-per-hour wind. (A knot is a nautical mile—6080 feet.) This relatively modest wind raises waves whose average height is five feet and whose energy is spread over a band of periods ranging from seven to ten seconds.

If the wind increases to thirty knots the waves become substantially higher and the periods longer. There is more energy available and these longer waves store it better. Now the average height is 13.6 feet and the maximum energy is centered around a period of twelve seconds.

The uppermost curve of the energy spectrum of forty-knot wind waves shows a sharp peak at 16.2 seconds; the average height of the waves has increased to twenty-eight feet.

Two things are clearly evident. As the wind velocity increases, (1) the amount of energy that can be stored by the waves increases greatly (this is because the waves are much higher and the energy is proportional to the square of the wave height), and (2) the periods become longer. (Note that in many papers dealing with waves, the period, T, has been replaced by its inverse, frequency. Thus $f = \dfrac{1}{T}$ and a ten-second wave has a frequency of 0.1.)

Table III gives the most important characteristics of seas that are fully developed for winds of various velocities. For example, a twenty-knot wind must blow for at least ten hours along a minimum fetch length of seventy-five miles to raise fully the waves it is capable of generating. When the sea from a twenty-knot wind is fully developed, the average height of the highest ten percent of the waves will be ten feet. If a fifty-knot wind were to blow for three days over a fifteen-hundred-mile fetch, the highest tenth of the waves would average about one hundred feet high.

TABLE III
CONDITIONS IN FULLY DEVELOPED SEAS

Wind	Distance	Time	Waves			
Velocity in knots	Length of fetch (nautical miles)	(hours)	Average height (feet)	H_3 significant height	H_{10} Average of the highest 10% (ft)	Period where most of energy is concentrated (sec)
10	10	2.4	0.9	1.4	1.8	4
15	34	6	2.5	3.5	5	6
20	75	10	5	8	10	8
25	160	16	9	14	18	10
30	280	23	14	22	28	12
40	710	42	28	44	57	16
50	1420	69	48	78	99	20

Fortunately for ships, storms rarely reach such dimensions or durations.

Even in storms with lower velocity winds there is always a statistical chance of a very high wave. No one can predict when or where or how high, but superwaves must exist because of the random nature of waves. For example, if one thousand waves were observed on twenty different occasions, on one of those occasions the highest of the thousand waves will be 2.22 times the significant height. Thus, if the significant height were forty-four feet, as it would be in a fully developed forty-knot sea, the exceptionally high wave could be ninety-seven feet high.

Such a wave could exist only momentarily in a storm and there it would be very unstable. It would tower over twice as high as most of its fellows, reaching upward into a mass of air moving at forty knots. The crest would then be blown off, forming a breaking wave in deep water. It is these breaking storm waves—and they need not be superwaves either—that do the serious damage to ships that are unlucky enough to be hit. The thousands of tons of violently moving water contained in the torn-off crest of even a moderate-sized breaking ocean wave can wipe the superstructure right off a ship.

The vast difference in the destructive power of breaking and non-breaking waves in deep water is worth examination since it illuminates a fundamental property of waves. Objects in the water, such as ships, tend to make the same motion as the water they displace. A ship at sea in large waves will describe orbital circles that are roughly the same size as the water in that part of the wave. There is little relative motion between the bulk of the ship and the surrounding water. This motion of a ship may be uncomfortable, but it is safe.

If the crest breaks off a wave, the water moves faster than the wave form and independently of the orbiting water (and ship). While moving in different directions the two may collide with disastrous results.

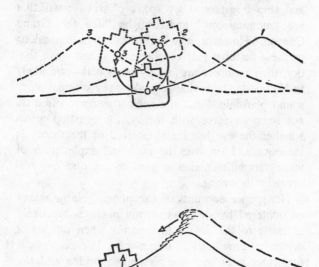

Fig. 20. Ship in breaking and non-breaking waves. *Top:* Ship and water particles in a large wave describe orbits of about the same size so that there is little relative motion. *Bottom:* Water in the crest of a large wave has broken free of the orbit and will collide violently with the ship.

GREAT STORM WAVES

When sailors talk about the sea it is not long before they are on the subject of storms, great waves, and ship disasters. They speak of wave crests that are "mountainous" and troughs "like the Grand Canyon." However, when asked to assign dimensions to these features that can be used to test wave theory, their numbers are mostly guesswork—and likely to be on the high side to make their original story sound plausible. Since the heights assigned often do not seem to agree with theory, the question arises whether the eye has been deceived or the theory is inadequate. Moreover the statistical explanation of wave variability makes it hard to say that any observation is wrong.

Newspaper accounts of exceptionally large waves encountered by ships on stormy passages are likely to relate to the deluge that occurs when the vessel drives her bow head-on into a wave. For example, if the water goes over the navigating bridge and the bridge is one hundred feet above the waterline, a hundred-foot wave is reported. The unexpected impact of even a few tons of broken or "white" water at that level is no doubt a fearsome occurrence worthy of mention, but it is not evidence of wave height. Even if the water were part of a wave (green water) the bridge is well forward of the ship's center, so that when the bow is down it is well below its proper level. The true wave height would be much less than one hundred feet.

When visibility is good and a large ship is on a

reasonably even keel, accurate estimates of wave height, even in a violent storm, are possible. The observer simply watches the distant horizon; when the crest of a wave obscures the horizon, that wave must be higher than the vertical distance between the observer's eye and the ship's waterline.

Stories of big waves at sea can be exciting. Vaughan Cornish, a British author who spent nearly half a century traveling the world on ships to collect data on waves, concluded that in North Atlantic storms waves over forty-five feet high were fairly common; he reported several well-authenticated examples of much larger ones. In his collection of data on wave length, he had many examples of storm waves six hundred to eight hundred feet from crest to crest, and swells two or three times that long.

In October 1921, the captain of the twelve-thousand-ton SS *Ascanius*, en route from Yokohama to Seattle, reported an extended storm of hurricane

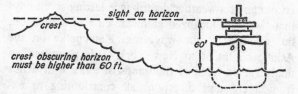

Fig. 21. Observing waves greater than sixty feet high from the SS *Ascanius*.

force in which the barometer went off the low end of the scale. He hove-to (stopped the ship) to ride it out and noted in the ship's log that when the ship was in the trough on an even keel, his eye was sixty feet above the water level alongside the ship. He was

57

certain some of the waves that obscured the horizon were greater than seventy feet high.

On December 29 of the following year, the SS *Majestic*, a large passenger liner, encountered a prolonged storm in the North Atlantic with winds of hurricane force and constant fierce rainsqualls. The ship was barely maintaining steerageway but "riding easily among waves of remarkable regularity and phenomenal size." Under these favorable observing conditions the ship's officers judged the waves and reported that the average height of a considerable number was around seventy-five feet and that individuals as high as ninety feet were seen.

There have been many reports of great waves at sea, but the one seen by the officers of the USS *Ramapo* and reported by Lieutenant Commander R. P. Whitemarsh in *The Proceedings of the U. S. Naval Institute* tops all the others by far. The *Ramapo*, a Navy tanker 478 feet long, was proceeding from Manila to San Diego, California, when it encountered a weather disturbance lasting seven days that "was not localized as in the case of a typhoon, but reached all the way from Kamchatka on the Asiatic continent to New York. This permitted an unobstructed fetch of thousands of miles with winds from a constant direction, all contributing to extremely high seas.

"By 2200 on February 6, 1933, there was a whole gale of 58 knots with mountainous seas. We maintained our easterly course with the wind almost directly astern. It would have been disastrous to have steamed on any other course.

"The storm reached its greatest height early the next morning when winds up to 68 knots were

58

clocked with the anemometer. Although the vessel was dwarfed in comparison with the seas, the conditions for observing the seas were ideal. There was practically no rolling and the pitching was easy; the moon was out astern. The period of the largest sea wave was 14.8 seconds as determined by stopwatch."

Among a number of separately determined observations, that of Lieutenant (j.g.) F. C. Margraff, the watch officer on the bridge, was selected as the most accurate. He declared that "while standing watch on the bridge he saw seas astern at a level above the main crow's nest and that at the moment of observation the horizon was hidden from view by the waves approaching from astern. Mr. Margraff is 5 feet 11¾ inches tall. The ship was not listed and the stern was in the trough of the sea."

On working out the geometry of the situation from the plans of the ship, as shown in Figure 22, the wave must have been at least one hundred and twelve feet high!

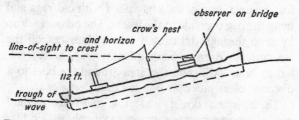

FIG. 22. How the *Ramapo* measured a wave one hundred and twelve feet high. (after Whitemarsh)

OIL ON TROUBLED WATERS

The calming effect of oil on the sea surface was known for many centuries before the physics of the action was understood. First, all oils are not equally effective; experience has shown that fish oils or other viscous animal oils are best and that petroleum products have relatively little effect. Since the latter are much more likely to be available around a modern boat, in recent years there have been many attempts to use motor oils without success. As a result, the idea of using oil to calm the sea surface has fallen into disrepute, to be regarded as an old seaman's tale without foundation in physics. But, properly used, oil can be very helpful to the small-boat operator under emergency conditions. However, he does not "pour" it on the troubled waters; rather he "leaks" it.

The time-honored method is to put cod-liver oil, for example, in a canvas bag filled with old rags and hang the bag overside in the water. The oil oozes drop by drop through the canvas and spreads out on the sea surface. Even a small quantity—say, a half gallon an hour—will calm the area around the boat to a distance of as much as one hundred feet.

There is no doubt whatever that this method works, but one must not expect too much. A thin film of oil could hardly be expected to have any effect on large waves or swell, but it does quickly extinguish the small waves. Moreover, as the sea surface becomes slick, the wind has less effect on it, no spray is blown about and the wave crests become more rounded. The boatman can see better and there is much less chance of a wave's breaking as its crest is blown off by the wind.

This smoothing is caused by increasing the surface tension of the nearby area of sea. Surface tension is a property of liquids that makes them act as though they were covered by an elastic film—something like a toy balloon filled with water. The higher the surface tension of the liquid, the stronger this invisible membrane acts. But since engineering handbooks give a surface tension for water twice that of oil, it is not readily apparent how the addition of oil can help matters.

The answer is that the surface tension of the oil increases as its thickness decreases. The thinner the film the better, for oil can act like an elastic membrane even when it is only a millionth of a millimeter thick. Thus, as the oil spreads away from the boat it becomes more effective, opposing any motion that tends to increase the surface area. At a distance from the boat depending on the velocity of the wind, the elastic limit of the increasingly thin film is exceeded. It breaks up and blows away, making it necessary continually to add more oil at the center.

Other materials that are mixed in the water or are floating on it also tend to reduce wave action. Extremely muddy water will cause waves to decay rapidly; so will masses of floating debris. Ice crystals formed by freezing sea water reduce wave height as do ice floes. For a hundred miles along the Southern California coast there is an almost continuous kelp bed parallel to the shore a few hundred yards off the beach. The large waves coming from far at sea pass through it unchanged, but the small waves caused by local winds are quickly dissipated, and the water surface is nearly always glassy just inside the kelp beds. In fact, one enterprising manufacturer now produces rubber kelp to reduce waves in small-boat harbors.

SWELL

As waves move out from under the winds that generated them, their character changes. The original wind waves are said to decay. The crests become lower, more rounded, and more symmetrical. They move in groups of similar period and height. Their form approaches that of a true sine curve. Such waves are now called swell, and in this form they can travel for thousands of miles across deep water with little loss of energy.

In more formal language, these waves are "periodic disturbances of the sea surface under the control of gravity and inertia and of such height and period as to break on a sloping shoreline."

The usual range of period of swell is from six to sixteen seconds, but occasionally longer periods are clocked. The average period of the swell arriving at the U.S. Pacific coast is slightly longer than measured in the Atlantic. This difference arises partly from the much greater size of the Pacific, in which more long waves can be generated in larger storm areas, and partly from the greater distances the waves must travel across the Atlantic continental shelf before they reach the shore—in which the longer period waves are attenuated.

As swell, the waves have relationships conforming

rather closely to the simple equations that applied in the wave channel. That is, their wave length is about $5.12\ T^2$ and they move at a speed of $\sqrt{\dfrac{gL}{2\pi}}$.

Table IV gives the range of wave lengths and velocities that swell in deep water would have if it were truly a sequence of regular sine waves. It is not, but this approximation seems to be the best that can be done at this time. The longest swell ever

TABLE IV
APPROXIMATE LENGTHS AND VELOCITIES OF SINUSOIDAL
SWELL IN DEEP WATER

(The final column, $d/L = 0.5$, is the depth at which each becomes a shallow water wave.)

T	$L = 5.12\ T^2$	$C = \sqrt{\dfrac{gL}{2\pi}}$	C	$d/L = 0.5$
Period in seconds	Wave length, feet	Velocity, feet/sec	Approximate velocity, miles/hr	Water depth, feet
6	184	30.5	21	92
8	326	40.6	28	163
10	512	51.0	35	256
12	738	61.0	42	369
14	1000	71.5	49	500
16	1310	82.0	56	655

reported, with a period of 22.5 seconds, came out of the south Atlantic and was measured by Vaughan Cornish on the Dover coast of England. These waves must have had a wave length of twenty-six hundred feet and a velocity of seventy-eight miles an hour.

For a rough estimate of wave lengths in deep water one can multiply the square of the period in seconds by five; to estimate the velocity (in miles per hour) multiply the period by 3.5.

Swell moves across the open ocean between the generating area and the distant shore in "trains" made up of groups of waves. These trains are bundles of energy. Although any wave in the group moves at a velocity that corresponds to its length as indicated above, the velocity of the group as a whole is only about half as fast. The explanation is: as the wave train moves into an undisturbed area it must use some of its forward-moving energy to set new water particles orbiting; this energy is contributed by the leading waves, with the result that these constantly disappear from the front of the advancing wave train; since new waves constantly form at the rear of the train, the number of waves and the total energy remain about the same, but the velocity of the group as a whole is reduced.

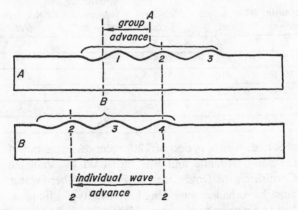

FIG. 23. Wave group advance. As the center of the wave group advances from *A* to *B*, wave number 1 dies out and wave number 4 forms behind. Since waves number 2 and 3 are moving at normal velocity, the velocity of a group of waves is only half that of the individual waves.

It is easy to see that the understanding of group velocity is most important to men who forecast the arrival of waves from distant storms. A wave group whose period averages twelve seconds will take two days to cross one thousand miles of open ocean instead of half that long, the speed of an individual twelve-second wave.

This phenomenon was first reported by J. Scott Russell in 1844, and it can be observed in a long wave channel if the wave-making machine is operated for only a few strokes. The observer, walking alongside the tank, focusing his attention on the first wave generated, will see it decrease in height and finally disappear altogether into the undisturbed water ahead of the group. The last wave in the group is usually not so clearly defined as the first, but sometimes a wave can be seen to develop behind the last wave generated.

Thus the composition of a group of waves is constantly changing and the individual waves observed at a shore are but remote descendants of those actually generated by a distant storm.

The energy possessed by a wave is of a twofold nature. In part it is kinetic energy, due to the motion of the water particles in their orbits; the remainder is potential energy due to the elevation of the center of gravity of the mass of water in the crest above sea level. For swell, the two energies are equal.

Eventually the deep-sea swell approaching a coast moves into the shallow water of the continental shelf, and when the depth of water is less than half the wave length, these waves feel bottom and undergo some radical changes in length, velocity, and direction.

Chapter IV

WAVES IN SHALLOW WATER

We have defined shallow-water waves as those that are traveling in water whose depth is less than half the wave length. Thus, whether a wave is in shallow water or not depends on the basin as well as on the wave. In a wave channel with water 2.5 feet deep, waves with periods longer than one sec-

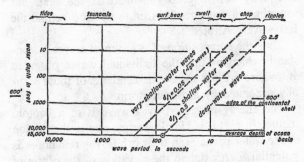

FIG. 24. Shallow-water waves.

ond are shallow-water waves; in six hundred feet of water at the edge of the continental shelf a sixteen-second wave is in shallow water, and in the deep ocean basin (average depth fifteen thousand feet) all waves with periods greater than eighty seconds are shallow-water waves.

Therefore, this chapter deals with the entire range of wave periods as illustrated in Figure 24. On the continental shelf, large ocean swell moves predominantly as shallow-water waves, and in the deep ocean, tsunamis and tides are very-shallow-water waves.

As these various waves approach shore and move across shallow water they react in special ways. They reflect, diffract, and refract—which means that they are turned back by vertical obstacles, spread their energy into the water behind projecting rocky promontories, and bend to fit a gradually shoaling bottom. The great low waves of the deep sea may move up an estuary with an abrupt steep-front or they may break down into a dozen smaller waves. On entering a bay or harbor they may excite it in such a way as to cause a sloshing motion.

In short, shallow-water waves have just as complicated characters as deep-water waves, and they are likely to be more interesting, because it is in shallow water that they most affect mankind.

REFLECTION

When a wave encounters a vertical wall such as a steep rocky cliff rising from deep water or the vertical end of a wave tank, it reflects back upon itself with little loss of energy. If the wave train is regular in period, a pattern of standing waves may be set up in which the orbits of the waves approaching the cliff and those reflected by it modify each other in such a way that there is only vertical water motion against the cliff and only horizontal motion at a distance out of one quarter wave length, much as shown in Figure 25. Regular wave trains are rare in

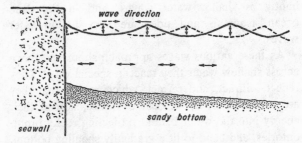

Fig. 25. Wave reflection (*clapotis*) from a nearly vertical wall. Standing wave patterns may be set up in which the water particles move as indicated.

nature and this unusual circumstance is called *clapotis*. The point is that as long as the wave is roughly sinusoidal, it exerts relatively little force on the structure that reflects it. Therefore, when possible, breakwaters are constructed in water too deep to cause waves to break. The forces that would be imposed on the same structure by breaking waves are far greater, as we will see presently.

Virtually any obstacle will reflect some part of the wave energy. An underwater barrier such as a submerged coral reef will cause reflections, even though the main waves seem to pass over it without much change. If the light is right, the reflections can be seen from the air as a halo of small waves surrounding the reef, bucking the main swell. Or, a steep beach may reflect waves to a remarkable extent— and as the reflected waves move outward and encounter the incoming waves head-on, thin sheets of

PLATE I. Dukw surfboarding on twelve-foot plunging breaker during a beach survey. (University of California)

PLATE II. Winter surf at Table Bluff, California. Breaker on the outermost bar (half a mile from the camera) is about twenty-five feet high. After breaking, the waves reform and break again on the inner bar. (University of California)

PLATE III. Close-up of an increasing swell and breaker. (Bascom)

PLATE IV. The surface of the sea is a complicated shape that makes it difficult to decide on wave height, length, or period. (Brown Brothers)

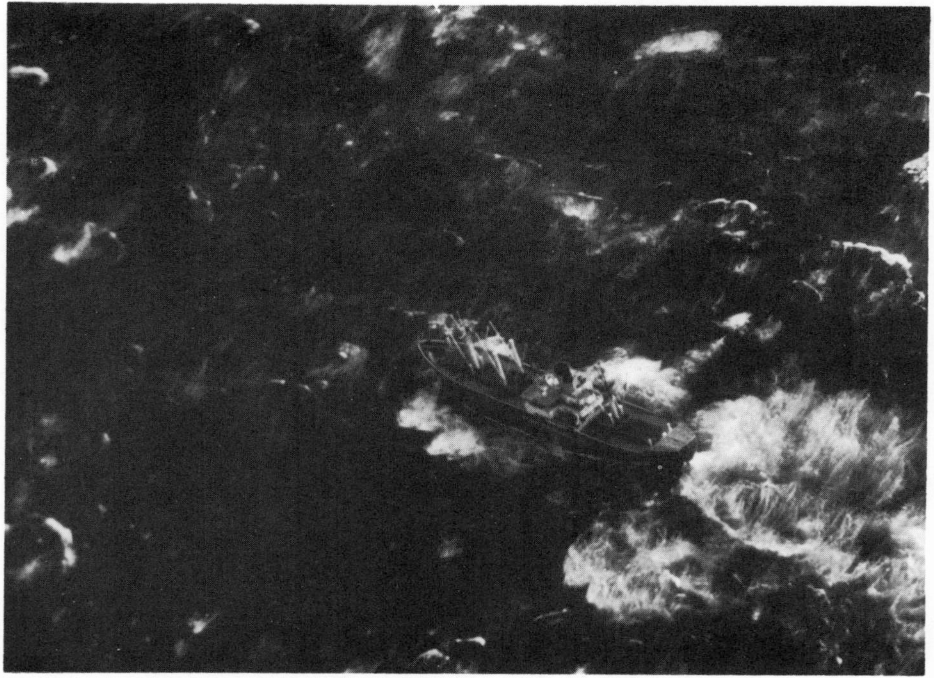

PLATE V. The surface of the sea during Hurricane Carol (1954) as it looked from the air to the Navy's "Hurricane Hunters." Winds of about a hundred miles an hour cause the wind streaks and haze. (U. S. Navy)

PLATE VI. Destroyer on the bounding main off the Virginia capes. The numbers on the bow are eight feet high. How big is the wave? (U. S. Navy)

PLATE VII. If you were on the bow of this ship would you describe these seas as mountainous? (The San Francisco *Examiner*)

PLATE VIII. An alert photographer aboard the *Brigham Victory* took these photos of the April 1, 1946, seismic sea wave destroying warehouses on the pier at Hilo, Hawaii. The unlucky longshoreman in the foreground died a moment later. (Wide World Photo)

PLATE IX. The tsunami of May 23, 1960, cleaned off several blocks of houses along the Hilo waterfront and deposited them inland as a line of driftwood. (Ichii, Honolulu *Advertiser*)

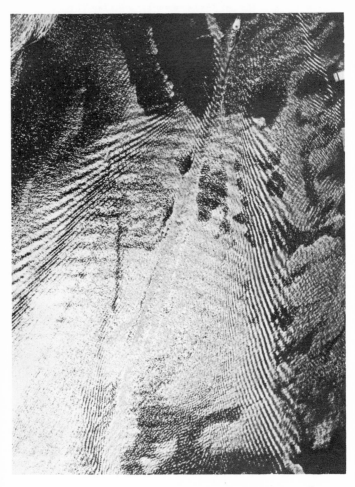

PLATE X. A complex wave system created by a moving ship can easily be seen in this photograph. (U. S. Navy)

PLATE XI. Long Beach, New Jersey, after the great storm of March 7–8, 1962. (Corps of Engineers)

PLATE XII. Sandspit in the harbor at Santa Barbara, California. Sand is moved along the coast from the left (west) by the wave-caused littoral current. In the quiet water created by the breakwater the sand stops moving, which creates problems both in the harbor and on the beaches to the east. (University of California)

water may shoot upward twenty feet or so. If the two meet at a slight angle a "zippering" effect is observed as the point of impact races along at as much as a hundred feet a second. The author has observed the waves of translation (foamlines) from large breakers strike steep cobble beaches and return seaward as reflected waves six feet high. When translatory waves of this size collide, there is a roar and much water is thrown about in confusion.

DIFFRACTION

Imagine that a train of waves (swell) moving across the ocean suddenly encounters a steep-sided island rising abruptly from the depths. Anyone would expect the waves to be lower on the lee side, and a boat seeking calmer water would run in behind the island. But exactly where would the boat stop rolling as it moved into more protected water?

Would the island cast a clear "wave shadow" in which the water is perfectly calm? The answer is no; the reason is that waves diffract. That is to say, as the waves pass the island some of their energy is propagated sidewise as the wave crest extends itself into the area apparently sheltered by the island.

Figure 26 shows what happens. When a train of regular waves passes an island whose geometric shadow is indicated by the dashed line B, some of the wave energy from the region between B and C flows along the crest into the region between B and A. The numbers given are approximate diffraction coefficients for this hypothetical case. That is, at C the waves are full height, at B they are only half the original height, and at A they are one tenth the height of C. The phenomena of wave diffraction must be taken into account by engineers who design breakwaters. Otherwise, ships moored inside, appar-

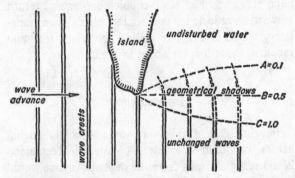

FIG. 26. Wave diffraction. As a train of waves passes a steep-sided island the wave energy originally concentrated between B and C is spread between A and C.

ently in a safe lee, might be damaged by wave action.

Diffraction need not be a shallow-water effect. This example specifies a steep-sided island rising abruptly from the depths. If the same waves had approached the island over a gently sloping underwater topography, the result would have been entirely different because of wave refraction.

REFRACTION

Refraction simply means bending. As waves move into shoaling water the friction of the bottom causes them to slow down, and those in shallowest water move the slowest. Since different segments of the wave front are traveling in different depths of water, the crests bend and wave direction constantly changes. Thus the wave fronts tend to become roughly parallel to the underwater contours.

A simple example, shown in Figure 69, is that of a set of regular waves approaching a straight shoreline

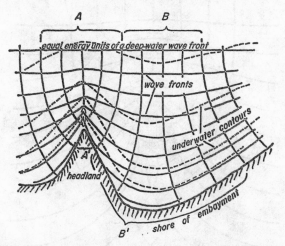

A   B

equal energy units of a deep-water wave front

wave fronts

underwater contours

headland

B'   *shore of embayment*

FIG. 27. Wave refraction causes a straight wave front in deep water to be bent until it almost parallels the shoreline. Equal energy units in deep water *A* and *B* are concentrated on the headland and spread along the bay shore. (Waves are moving toward the shore.)

at an angle. The inshore part of each wave is moving in shallower water, and consequently moves slower, than the part in deep water. The result is that the wave fronts tend to become parallel to the shoreline. Thus an observer on the beach always sees the larger waves come in directly toward him even

71

though some distance out from shore they are seen to be approaching at an angle. The effect of refraction is to concentrate wave energy against headlands as shown in Figure 27; consequently it is a process of considerable geological significance. It is a modern

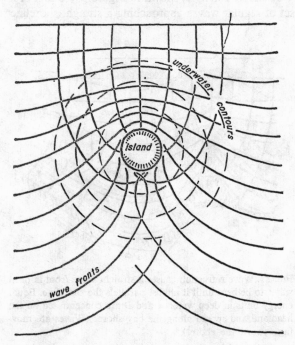

FIG. 28. Wave refraction around a circular island. (Waves are moving down the page.)

expression of the old sailor's saying, "The points draw the waves." Figure 6 in Chapter I shows the result of wave refraction acting over a long period of time.

Even on a circular island (with a gently sloping underwater topography on all sides) a wave train from one direction will "wrap itself" around the island so that the wave fronts arrive nearly parallel to the beaches on all sides, although of course the waves are substantially higher on the side facing directly into the deep-sea swell.

As train of swell becomes a shallow-water wave group where the depth is less than half the wave length, the effects of refraction begin. One can compute the velocity of a wave in shallow water, and it is possible to make a diagram showing how far the various parts of a wave advance during a series of equal time intervals. Such refraction diagrams are very useful in visualizing how waves of various periods and directions will influence a shoreline or a proposed coastal structure.

There are several methods of drawing refraction diagrams; all begin with an accurate contour chart of the bottom configuration out to a depth of half the longest wave that will be considered. Then the period and direction of the waves to be diagramed must be selected. The practicing coastal engineer will prepare diagrams for waves of many periods and directions, but usually he will also make a statistical wave hindcast. That is, he will make estimates of wave heights and periods based on historic weather maps to obtain statistics on what waves have arrived in the past and are likely to arrive in the future. One of these waves is likely to be predominant, and he will start with it—on much of the U.S. West Coast it is often a twelve-second wave from the northwest. Now he proceeds by drawing a straight line representing a wave front in deep water, or using another method, a wave ray (perpendicular to the wave front) that shows the direction of wave advance. In the wave-front method it is customary to calculate the new, somewhat reduced wave length for each contour depth and to use these to step off the advance of the wave front. The resulting diagram shows the successive positions of the wave front at time intervals equal to the period. As the wave slows down the wave fronts get closer and closer together.

The principal question answered by a refraction diagram is: How is the wave energy distributed when it reaches the coast? If the deep-water wave front is divided into equal parts and wave rays are drawn through these perpendicular to each wave front, the energy distribution is readily seen. These wave rays separate areas of equal wave energy and are called orthogonals. The ratio of the length of the wave crest between orthogonals in deep water to that at the beach is the refraction coefficient. With it, one can compare the amounts of wave energy reaching various points along the coast and determine the effectiveness of proposed breakwaters.

A case history illuminating this method of using swell hindcasting and refraction diagrams to determine how waves damaged a shoreline structure is the study made by M. P. O'Brien in 1947. During the period April 20–24, 1930, large breakers damaged a short segment of the tip of the Long Beach, California, breakwater. This incident was unusual because the breakwater had withstood wave attack for years; at the time of the failure local winds were light and the sea offshore—observed from gambling ships anchored just beyond the three-mile limit—was calm. At the San Pedro Breakwater, only a few miles to the north, there were no breakers; on the beaches to the south, lifeguards noticed no unusual wave activity. Nevertheless the waves breaking against the tip of the breakwater dislodged stones ranging in weight

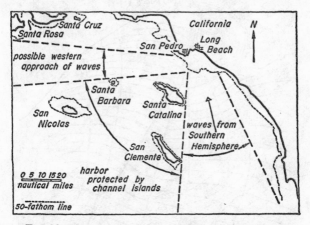

FIG. 29. Wave approaches to Long Beach, California.

from four to twenty tons. Observers had estimated the period of these waves at twenty to thirty seconds —a very-long-period swell.

Seventeen years later O'Brien set about finding out why. Historical weather maps were consulted, and it was found that at the time two storm centers in the Northern Hemisphere existed that might have been capable of producing long-period waves; one was to the west, the other to the northwest. No weather data from the Southern Hemisphere were available. The configuration of the coast and the protection of the channel islands immediately excluded the northwest storm as a possible wave source; a

75

refraction diagram for twenty-second waves for the storm from the west showed that its waves could not have produced the observed effect either. Thus both

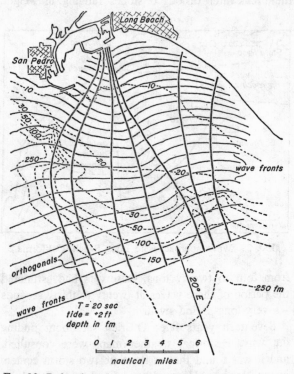

Fig. 30. Refraction diagram for destructive waves at Long Beach, California, showing how underwater topography several hundred feet deep and a dozen miles offshore focused wave energy on the breakwater.

the known storms were ruled out, and it was concluded that the source of the waves that damaged the breakwater must have been somewhere in the Southern Hemisphere, outside the area covered by the weather maps.

To the southeast the harbor area does not have the protection of offshore islands, and so a refraction diagram was constructed for twenty-second waves from various southerly directions. It was then discovered that a hump in the underwater topography, 180 to 600 feet deep and ten miles away, acted as a lens to focus waves coming from S 20° E on the breakwater tip; that is, a special refraction condition for that particular wave period caused the wave energy of several miles of crest to converge. Waves only two feet high in deep water had been concentrated in a narrow zone as breakers over twelve feet high, and they caused the damage.

STORM SURGES

During a violent storm there may be a substantial rise in the sea level along a coast that is known as a "storm tide" or surge. When this happens the wind-raised storm waves are superimposed on this surge, and sometimes the land is invaded with disastrous effect. This rise in water level is often the combined result of an atmospheric low pressure area surrounded by high pressure areas offshore; that is, the differences in air pressure cause a hump in the sea surface under the low pressure area. As the storm moves toward land this hump of water invades coastal areas. In addition, the strong winds create large waves and drive them across shoaling water, piling them on the shore. These steep, breaking waves are driven so hard, one upon another, that they create a general landward-flowing surface current (mass transport plus translation) that moves faster than the surplus water can return seaward along the bottom. The result of both factors is a flooded coast. The battering waves atop the general flood cause the serious destruction, for shoreline structures are now in the surf zone.

Some case histories of the great destructive effect of such surges serve to remind us of how quietly the ocean usually lies in its basin and how damaging a small change in sea level can be.

Probably the most famous example of a storm surge was the Galveston, Texas, "flood" of 1900. On that occasion a hurricane with winds of one hundred and twenty miles an hour raised the water level along that shore of the Gulf of Mexico fifteen feet above the usual two-foot tidal range. The storm waves, probably another twenty-five feet high, rode in atop the storm tide and demolished the city; some five thousand people drowned. A similar situation was created by Hurricane Carla of 1961 which also struck along the Gulf coast. But in the intervening years progress in weather and wave research made it possible to predict such surges. The area was evacuated in advance of its arrival so that there was no loss of life and minimum destruction.

On February 1, 1953, a strong gale swept down the North Sea and piled its waters against the Dutch coast. The storm surge rose ten feet above the highest high-tide level; the waves topped the dikes. The overflowing water eroded gulleys in the unsheathed inner side of the dikes until they were breached in sixty-seven places. In a short time channels as deep as one hundred feet and fifteen hundred feet wide were cut in the dikes. As the sea defenses collapsed, the North Sea poured in, and a steep-fronted wave advanced across the low country. The result was that 800,000 acres were flooded, 1783 people drowned and the damage exceeded $250 million. But in a few years the Dutch had repaired the dikes, reclaimed their land, and were extending the dike system to include new lands. This super-gale was later deter-

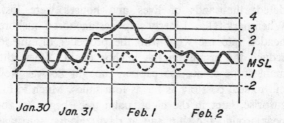

FIG. 31. Storm surge record made by tide gauge at Rotterdam, Holland, compared with the predicted tide. On February 1, 1953, the water level reached 2.75 meters (nine feet) above high tide and was largely responsible for the breaching of the dikes.

mined by Dutch engineers to have been a "four-hundred-year storm." That is, the chance that all the unfavorable circumstances (high winds of long duration in that direction) would occur at one time was such that there was a likelihood of similar occurrence only once in four hundred years. Almost nobody expected the occurrence of such a storm.

India's low flat shores along the Bay of Bengal are densely populated and have at various times been invaded by great storm surges which have taken a terrible toll of life. In 1876 the rising water accompanying a single storm caused more than two hundred thousand deaths. More recently, on October 31, 1960, at Chittagong, Pakistan, near the mouth of the Ganges, a cyclone and storm surge caused much damage but not without some amusing side effects. At its worst, the winds were one hundred and twenty miles an hour and the sea surface suddenly rose twenty-two feet—inadvertently recorded by means of a high-water mark left on the wall inside a lighthouse tower. Three small islands were completely inundated; thousands of lives and houses were lost. When dark fell, a Liberty ship was anchored offshore headed into the wind with the propeller turning to reduce the strain on the anchor chain. When the main surge came, the captain thought he was well out to sea, possibly as far as four miles. Much to his surprise, later in the night, palm trees began to appear around the ship and at daybreak the ship was found to be resting on the ground about a mile inland. The ship could not be moved and was subsequently cut up for scrap.

The captain of another ship recorded the storm in his log in some detail, including: "At 1407 a tidal wave estimated to be forty feet high bore down on this vessel and swept completely over her from bow to stern. The floodlights on the foremast and the fashion boards on top of the flying bridge wheelhouse washed away. In the midst of the mountainous seas this tidal wave was a distinct entity, operating as a separate unit." He closes, "Why did I ever sell the farm to go to sea?"

Khalilur Rahman, a Pakistan meteorological observer stationed at the airport, also noted the surge in his log: "Tidal bore opened the door and entered the observatory room at 1314 filling it with sea water. Giving up all hope of life I shut the door, otherwise the properties of the Government would go away with the current of sea water. Whole night I was standing on a chair, placing it on the table to read the barometer. It was impossible to read the barometer after 1400 as I could not move with four to six feet of water on the ground. I like to mention here that the lower portion of the barometer was under water for some time."

The New England coast has had many serious storm surges and sixty-three hurricanes have been recorded since the Pilgrims landed. Of these, twelve (one every twenty-five years) have caused serious tidal flooding and major losses of life and property. The most spectacular example in recent history is that of Hurricane Carol, in August 1954. On that occasion the water level at Providence, Rhode Island, rose sixteen feet above normal, flooding the downtown business area eight feet deep and causing losses of $41 million. Providence officials decided to take action and build a protective tidal barrier rising 22.5 feet above mean sea level across the upper end of Narragansett Bay. Although the structure will cost some $17 million, the savings in average annual storm surge damage are expected to equal the cost of the structure in three years.

Chapter V

TIDES AND SEICHES

The study of the tides is a large and complicated subject, most of which is beyond the scope of this book. The tides, however, are an important form of long-period wave, and it would be illogical to ignore them entirely. Besides, they play an important part in beach and coastal processes because they constantly change the depth of water in which waves approach the coast and the level at which waves strike the beach. Therefore, we shall touch lightly on the main points and encourage the especially interested reader to dig into the references for more detailed information and a fuller explanation.

THE TIDES

On all seacoasts there is a rhythmic rise and fall of the water which is called the tide, and associated with this vertical movement of the water surface are horizonal motions of the water known as tidal currents. Together they are known as the tides.

Tides are the longest waves oceanographers commonly deal with, having a period of forty-three thousand seconds (twelve hours and twenty-five minutes) and a wave length of half the circumference of the earth. The crest and trough of the wave are known as high tide and low tide. The wave height is called the range of tide, but since it is measured only in places where it is influenced by the shape of the shore, it varies greatly from place to place.

The gravitational attraction of the moon and the sun on the earth and the waters cause tides. Long before a word for gravity existed, the ancients must have realized vaguely that there was some connection between the moon and the motion of the water. But our civilization developed on the shores of the Mediterranean, an essentially tideless sea. Not until a number of explorers had ventured beyond the Gates of Hercules into the Atlantic and observed tides in England, where the range is large, was the relationship between the phases of the moon and the height of the tide established. Then some fifteen hundred years passed before Johannes Kepler wrote of "some kind of magnetic attraction between the moon and the earth's waters"—and Galileo scoffed.

It remained for Isaac Newton to discover the law of gravity, which holds that the gravitational attraction between two objects is directly proportional to their masses and inversely proportional to the square of the distance between them. From this relationship it can be shown that the gravitational attraction of the sun for the earth is about one hundred and fifty times that of the moon. The tremendous mass of the sun more than makes up for its much greater distance. But the moon is the primary cause of tides. Why?

The answer is that the difference in attraction for water particles at various places on the earth is far more important than total attraction. That is, because of the moon's very nearness (average only 239,000 miles) there is a big difference in the gravitational attraction from one side of the earth to the other.

The water on the side of the earth nearest the moon is some four thousand miles closer to the moon than the center of the earth; the water on the far side is four thousand miles farther away. The sun, however, is ninety-three million miles away, and a few thousand miles one way or the other make comparatively little difference. Thus, the sun's gravitational force, although far larger, does not change very much from one side of the earth to the other. So the moon is more important in producing tides. For the sake of simplicity much of the following discussion speaks only of the effect of the moon, but the sun's effect is similar.

The result of these differences in gravitational attraction is that two bulges of water are formed on the earth's surface, one toward the moon, the other, as we shall see, away from it. The earth rotates on its axis once a day, and it is not difficult to imagine that it turns constantly inside a fluid envelope of ocean whose watery bulges are supported by the moon. This concept considers the tide wave to be standing still while the ocean basin turns beneath it. Thus, most points on earth experience two high tides and two low tides a day.

It is easy to see why the gravitational attraction of the moon should raise a bulge of water on the side of the earth toward the moon, but it is not quite so easy to understand why there should be a similar bulge on the opposite side, away from the moon. Let me try to clarify that point.

TIDES AND SEICHES

If the earth vanished, leaving three particles in space at distances corresponding to the center and opposite sides of the earth, the moon's gravity would act on them just the same. If we draw vector arrows from each point toward the moon, with lengths representing the intensities of gravitational attraction, the one nearest the moon is longest and the one farthest away is shortest.

But the three points are in fact part of the earth, which remains at a fixed distance from the moon because of the centrifugal effect of the rotating earth-moon system. If this force is represented at each point by an arrow equal in length but opposite in direction to that at the center of the earth, the

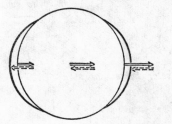

Fig. 32. Tide-producing forces.

remaining force and direction will be equivalent to the tide-producing force. The differences in length between each of the pairs of arrows shown in Figure 32 correspond in magnitude and direction to the forces producing the tidal bulges on opposite sides of the earth.

The moon rotates about the earth (in the same direction as the earth's rotation) completing an orbit once a month. This motion of the moon requires any

85

point on earth to go slightly farther than one revolution to come beneath the moon again; thus, the tidal day is twenty-four hours and fifty minutes long.

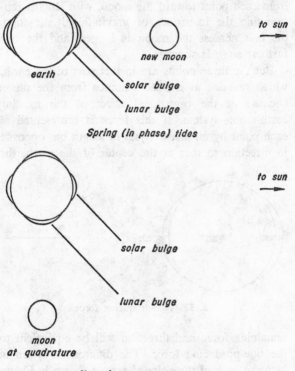

FIG. 33. Spring and neap tides.

One further complexity is that the bulge does not come directly beneath the moon but is slightly ahead of it as shown in Figure 34. This positioning is the

86

result of the friction of the earth as it rotates beneath the water. The rough-bottomed ocean basins tend to drag the bulges along; the gravitational effect of the moon tends to hold the bulge beneath it. The result is a compromise position at which these two forces are in equilibrium. In consequence a point on earth passes beneath the moon *before* high tide.

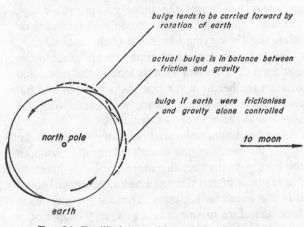

FIG. 34. Equilibrium position of the tidal bulge.

The sun tides, though much smaller, are important because of the way they increase and reduce the lunar tides. The two most important situations are when the earth, sun, and moon are aligned (in phase) and when the three make a right angle (out of phase).

In the in-phase case the solar bulge rides on top of the lunar bulge to make spring tides. During spring tides, which have nothing to do with the spring season but occur about every two weeks, the water level rises higher and falls lower than usual. This large range of tide lasts two or three days; then the two bulges get progressively further out of phase until, a week later, the high and low tides are about twenty percent less than average. These are neap tides; in effect, the sun's gravitational force reduces the moon's bulges.

Between these two extremes the solar bulge adds in a way that warps the shape of the main bulge, and the high and low tides come a little earlier or later, slightly varying the length of the tidal day.

Armed with this information, we are much better equipped than ancient man to look at the moon and forecast the height of the tide. At new moon and full moon there are spring tides; neaps come when the moon is in the first or last quarter.

Another important variation in the height of the tide is the result of the moon's elliptical orbit about the earth. At perigee, the nearest point in its orbit, the moon is fifteen thousand miles closer; at apogee it is that much farther away. This change in distance (and therefore in the attractive force) causes tides that are, respectively, twenty percent higher and lower than average. Perigee is reached once an orbit (once a month) and only rarely does this coincide with the in-phase alignment of sun, earth, and moon. But at least twice a year both effects exist at the same time—that is, a full moon or a new moon exists at perigee. Then the perigee tides add to the spring tides to produce the highest tides of the year.

Having considered the main forces that produce tides, we now can think about how these curious waves behave. Many shores, including the U.S. Atlantic coast, experience two tides a day of about equal heights; these are called semidiurnal (semi-daily). A few places in the world have only one high and one low a day. And most of the Pacific and Indian Oceans have mixed tides; that is, the heights of high and low waters are unequal, as at Seattle or Ketchikan.

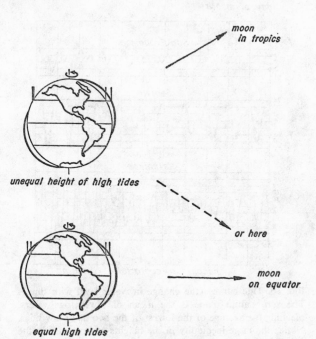

FIG. 35. Tidal inequality.

The cause of this changing inequality is shown in Figure 35. When the moon is opposite the equator the highs and lows are about equal. But when the moon is "in the tropics"—that is, above the tropics

89

of Cancer or Capricorn—different thicknesses of bulge move past points away from the equator.

One of the most important influences on the height and character of the tide is the shape of the basin where it is observed. No good measurements have

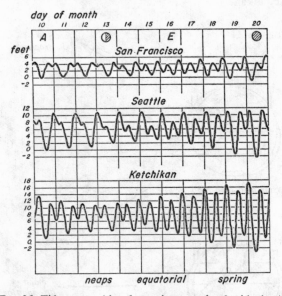

FIG. 36. Tide curves (the change in water level with time). The zero datum plane is the mean of lower low waters, meaning the average of the lowest of the two daily low tides. Notice the large inequality in the heights of low tides in the same day except when the moon is on the equator. The large range of tides are spring tides; the small range are the neaps.

yet been made of the height of the tide in the deep ocean. There the range is believed to be small, perhaps a foot, as it is on small mid-ocean islands.

But as the solid earth turns beneath the tidal bulge,

the shallow continental shelf acts as though it were a wedge driven under the wave front. The result is that the deep-water tidal range is much exaggerated at the shore. Estuaries with wide funnel-like openings into the ocean tend to amplify the tide range further. The width of the tide wave that enters the opening is restricted as the channel narrows; this constriction concentrates the wave energy and increases its height. Of course, if the estuary is very long, the frictional effects of sides and bottoms gradually reduce the height of the tide wave until it vanishes.

The importance of coastal configuration is illustrated by the difference in tidal height between Nantucket Island (about a foot) and the Bay of Fundy (over forty feet) which are only a few hundred miles apart. The opposite ends of the Panama Canal are only about fifty airline miles apart, but there is a great difference in the tides at the two terminals. At Colón, on the Caribbean side, the tide is generally diurnal and the range is about a foot; at Balboa, on the Pacific side, the tides are semidiurnal with an average height of fourteen feet and the locks are built to withstand spring tides of as much as twenty-one feet. This difference will create some interesting problems when a sea-level canal finally is built.

Although the tide doubtless advances across the ocean like a sine wave, there are only a few places on earth where this pattern can be observed directly. One such location is Chesapeake Bay. There the troughs and crest (the high and low tides) move up the bay as a series of "progressive" waves traveling slowly at "square root of gd" velocity. Usually there are two high-tide zones within its 150-mile length at the same time, with fifty miles of low-tide water in between.

It is interesting to speculate on the tide waves that must forever circle about Antarctica. From such speculation the "progressive wave" or "southern ocean" tide theory originated. The idea is simply that the Antarctic Ocean is a continuous belt of water extending completely around the earth, six hundred miles wide at its narrowest point. The tidal bulges must act as a forced wave into which energy is constantly being added by the tide-producing forces. As each high tide passes the openings into the Indian, South Atlantic, and the South Pacific, waves are initiated that travel freely northward and modify the local tides as they go.

Accompanying the rise and fall of the tide are substantial horizontal motions of water known as tidal currents. Like the vertical changes they have little significance in the open sea, but in harbors and narrow estuaries they are of considerable importance. On a rising tide the currents are said to be flooding; on a falling tide, they ebb. The direction of flow is the set of the current.

When there is no flow, the current is slack; thus the time of slack water is usually within an hour of high or low water. The maximum current velocity comes about at the same time as the maximum change in the height of the water. Since these relationships depend largely on the local conditions, no general rule applies.

Tidal currents of ten knots in Seymour Narrows, Alaska, and four knots in the Golden Gate to San Francisco Bay are normal. Such currents have little influence on open beaches, but they may have considerable effect on sand movements in and near harbor mouths. For example, the combined effect of these currents and of ocean wave forces often causes a sandy bar (harbor bar) to form just outside the harbor entrance. This barrier will cause large waves to break and endanger small craft entering or leaving the harbor, thus explaining the many allusions in literature to sailors' fears of a breaking or moaning bar.

Tidal or other currents will cause waves to break or shorten their wave length. It is this change in the texture of the sea surface that permits the Gulf Stream and other great currents to be recognized from the air.

Sea level is the height that the sea surface would assume if it were undisturbed by waves, tides, or winds. But because these disturbances do exist, the technique of averaging all possible sea levels has been adopted. The result is mean sea level (MSL), a convenient datum plane from which heights of tide or depths of water on a chart are measured. Charts and tide tables for the U.S. Pacific coast refer to another datum: mean of lower low waters (MLLW)— the average height of the lowest of two low tides a day.

TIDAL BORES

There are a number of places in the world where rivers enter the ocean via long funnel-shaped bays. In such estuaries, especially during high spring tides, the broad front of the incoming tide wave is restricted by the narrowing channel and the shoaling water so that it abruptly increases in height and a visible wave front or bore exists. Most bores are dull (except to the ardent wave researcher) and are regarded merely as a local curiosity, but in a few places they are respected or even feared.

Sir George Airy, one of the founders of wave theory, observed the bore in the Severn River in England and wrote that he was thrilled by "the visible advancing front of that great solitary wave," the tide.

Actually, on entering shallow water the solitary wave front often breaks down into a series of small waves. Photos of the Severn bore show a series of about six or eight short steep waves about a foot high and ten feet long moving up a small glassy-surfaced river. In other places the entry of the tidal water causes the river surface to heave upward with an almost imperceptible front; in the space of two minutes the water level rises by three feet or more.

A few famous bores have steep breaking fronts that connect the original water surface with a new surface at a substantially higher level. That of the Chien-Tang River in northern China has been described by Commander W. U. Moore, R.S.: "At Haining, where there is a sudden contraction of the channel, the bore is eight to eleven feet high, extending in a nearly straight line across the river which is rather more than one statute mile in width, traveling between twelve and thirteen knots, its front a cascade of bubbling foam falling forward and pounding on itself. The slope of this traveling cascade is uniform at any particular part of the front, but varies in different places from 40° to 70°, being highest and steepest over the deep parts of the river."

Visitors to the Hankow waterfront have been

amazed to see the local boatmen suddenly paddle frantically for the riverbank and apparently without cause pull their boats out of a placid stream. In a few minutes the breaking bore passes, the boats are returned to the river at its new, higher level and work resumes.

The bore of the Amazon is even more spectacular and is said to attain a height of twenty-five feet. Seen from the high dikes near the river mouth it has the appearance of a several-miles-long waterfall traveling upstream at a speed of twelve knots for three hundred miles. The roar can be heard for fifteen miles.

SEICHING

If the surface of an enclosed body of water such as a lake or bay is disturbed, long waves may be set up which will rhythmically slosh back and forth as they reflect off opposite ends. These waves, called seiches, have a period that depends on the size and depth of the basin. They are a rather common phenomenon, but because the wave height is so low and the length so long, they are virtually invisible, and few laymen are aware of their existence.

Seiches can be regarded as standing-wave patterns or as the reflection of trapped waves. A pattern of standing waves (in contrast to the progressive waves of the open ocean) is composed of nodes, at which the height of the water surface stays the same, and loops, where the surface moves up and down. The nodes and loops maintain a fixed position, as do the surface particles of water, but beneath the surface there are swift currents as the water shifts to support the changing wave form.

Natural basins are so irregular in shape and depth that it is best to begin by thinking about the nice clean situation that exists in a bathtub. A tub is nearly rectangular and has almost vertical friction-less sides—thus fulfilling the requirements of simple theory. If you put about six inches of water in your tub you can make model standing waves or seiches.

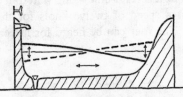

fundamental

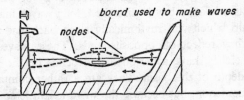
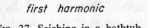

first harmonic

FIG. 37. Seiching in a bathtub.

First set the mass of water rocking with a funda-mental wave that reflects back and forth off each end. The midpoint of the tub is a node and the water depth there will remain the same (six inches) while that at each end will vary from, say, four inches to eight inches. If you add some neutrally buoyant marker, such as small wads of paper that float at mid-depth and move with the water particles, the motion of the water in these standing waves becomes apparent. Beneath the nodes there are high horizontal velocities; at the extremities the motion is mainly vertical. The period will be about two seconds. The fundamental period is that of a wave whose length is twice the distance between reflecting boundaries.

Now float a piece of board crossways at the midpoint and pump it up and down at a rate of about once a second. The water in the tub will now resonate in a different fashion. There will be two nodes and three loops. This is the first harmonic.

These measured periods confirm the simple formula for the natural period of a closed basin. $T_n = \dfrac{2l}{(n+1)\sqrt{gd}}$ in which l is the length of the tub —about four feet, $\sqrt{gd}$ is the velocity of a long wave ($\sqrt{32 \times 0.5} = 4$); n is the "order" of motion (fundamental $= 0$, 1st harmonic $= 1$, etc.).

Thus the natural period of the tub is two seconds and its first harmonic is one second. For a harbor a mile across averaging fifty feet deep the fundamental period is 264 seconds and the first harmonic 132 seconds. Other, higher harmonic orders may also be present at the same time.

Since few harbors have the neat boundaries of a bathtub, the waves do not reflect evenly and it might be expected that long wave patterns would be difficult to establish. Not so. Even harbors with exceedingly irregular shapes seem to rock with remarkable regularity, which is recorded on the tide gauges. Moreover, many harbors and bays have a large part of one side open to the ocean. This has two major effects: (1) The laws governing the seiching are different and (2) disturbances from the ocean can easily enter and start the harbor seiching.

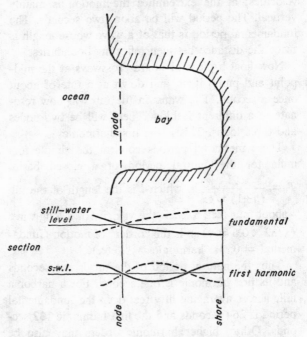

Fig. 38. Seichding in an open-sided bay. Natural period $= T_n = \dfrac{4l}{(n+1)\sqrt{gd}}$ (Note that an independent set of seiches may reflect back and forth across the bay in the other direction.)

If one side of the bay is open to the ocean, the missing reflecting surface is replaced by a nodal line as shown in Figure 38. Then the fundamental mode of oscillation is that in which the opening is at the first node; the first harmonic has the second node at the opening.

Tidal recordings made on open coasts also show seiche-like motions of the water surface that can be interpreted only as oscillations of the water masses on the continental shelf. These are believed to exist because the shelf acts like an open bay. Thus we discover that neither the bathtub nor the bay is necessary for this kind of wave to exist.

The question now arises as to the source of the disturbance that causes seiching. In a lake or other completely enclosed basin a sudden change in atmospheric pressure, such as would be caused by a wind-squall passing over one end, is the most likely cause. But seiching in bays that open into the ocean is almost invariably caused by the arrival of a long-period

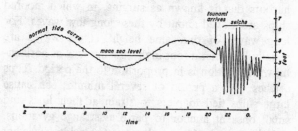

FIG. 39. Seiche in Pago Pago, Samoa, excited by the tsunami of May 22, 1960.

wave train. A Pacific tsunami will usually succeed in exciting all the bays and harbors around its rim. Often these will oscillate for days, producing tide-gauge records similar to that shown in Figure 39 of Pago Pago, Samoa, on May 22, 1960.

Once the water is set in motion by the first arriving wave, seiching at the natural period of the harbor is likely to mask subsequent wave arrivals, thus making it difficult to obtain the period of the tsunami itself from the tide gauge. At Pago Pago, for example, the natural period of the harbor is twenty-two minutes and its precise rhythmic motion is quite unlike that of other harbors disturbed by the same tsunami. If, by coincidence, the period of the tsunami is an even multiple of the natural period of the harbor, then the seiching motion is amplified by each new wave that arrives, and the water motion inside the harbor may become more violent than the motion outside. The fact that tsunamis are relatively rare suggests that long-period waves from other causes are responsible for creating most seiches.

The phenomenon of seiching is rarely troublesome to man, the exception being a situation in some harbors that is known as surging, in which moored ships are moved about by these long low waves. For long waves of the same height (these waves are usually less than a foot high) the amount of horizontal water motion is in proportion to the period. Thus seiches with a period of several minutes can cause large ships tied to piers to strain at their lines and small ones at anchor to perform strange gyrations.

It is not easy for an observer to decide just what effect these waves have on ships or other floating objects because the motion is slow. Therefore, in 1946, the author, while studying surging in Monterey harbor, took time-lapse pictures of the fishing fleet at anchor in the bay. The boats were tethered to moving buoys by a single bowline and thus were reasonably free to move. A rigidly supported motion picture camera set up on the bluff over the harbor was used to take pictures of the boats at the rate of one frame per second. When these photographs were projected at sixteen frames per second the surging motion was speeded up sixteen times. Clear patterns of water motion became evident as the previously indiscernible three-minute surge was compressed into eleven seconds. Later on, boats in the relatively quiet Noyo River and Santa Barbara harbors were similarly photographed on days when no surging motion could be observed. To our surprise, when the film was projected and the boat motion speeded up, a substantial surge could be seen. The boats would strain on their lines in unison first in one direction and then in the other with remarkable regularity.

In most harbors the surging is more a scientific curiosity than a serious problem, but Los Angeles harbor is an exception. There, even when the water surface appears calm, large ships tied up may move as much as ten feet, snapping heavy mooring lines, breaking piles, and damaging the ships themselves. These invisible surges have periods of three, six, and twelve minutes, corresponding to the natural periods of the basin.

When the tsunami of April 1, 1946, arrived with a period of about fifteen minutes, this was close enough to the natural period so that each new wave that arrived added to the height of the existing ones in the harbor. Fortunately there were not many waves in the series, and, somewhat surprisingly, no unusual damage was reported by the larger vessels.

Chapter VI

IMPULSIVELY GENERATED WAVES

When a force is suddenly applied to a water surface, waves are generated. The impulse of a pebble tossed into a puddle sends out a train of waves in concentric circles. In the ocean an earthquake, a volcanic eruption, a landslide or a nuclear explosion may produce the same effect on a much larger scale. The train of waves leaving such an event often contains a huge amount of energy and moves at high speed. As a result the waves may be tremendously destructive when they encounter a populated shore.

The general public has long referred to these waves as tidal waves, much to the annoyance of American oceanographers who are acutely aware that there is no connection with the tides. In an effort to straighten out the matter they adopted the Japanese word tsunami, which now is in general use. Later they discovered that tsunami merely means tidal wave in Japanese, but at least the annoyance has been shifted overseas.

SEISMIC SEA WAVES

A somewhat more descriptive term that applies to waves caused by earthquakes is seismic sea waves.

There are several mechanisms by means of which earthquakes can generate seismic sea waves, two of which are illustrated. The first is a simple fault in which tension in the submarine crustal rock is relieved by the abrupt rupturing of the rock along an inclined plane. When such a fault occurs, a large mass of rock drops rapidly and the support is removed from a column of water that extends to the surface. The water surface oscillates up and down as

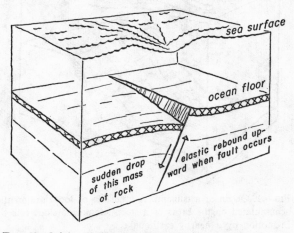

FIG. 40. Origin of a tsunami. A fault in the crustal rock causes part of the sea floor to drop rapidly. The water surface above also falls and a series of seismic sea waves are generated.

it seeks to return to mean sea level, and a series of waves is sent out. If the rock fails in compression, the mass of rock on one side rides up over that on the other, and a column of water is lifted, but the result is the same: a tsunami.

103

A second mechanism is a landslide, which is set in motion by an earthquake. If the slide begins above water, abruptly dumping a mass of rock into the sea, waves are made by the same action as the plunger in the wave channel. An example of such an event will presently be cited. If the slide occurs well below the surface, it creates waves as shown in Figure 41. Both

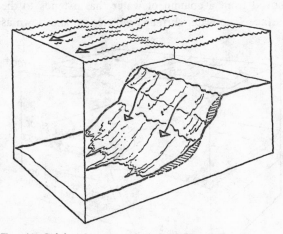

FIG. 41. Origin of a tsunami. A landslide of loose sediment accumulated on the brow of a steep submarine slope is set in motion by a nearby earthquake.

drawings are much exaggerated in order to make the point. Actually the water surface may fall only a few feet in water many thousands of feet deep, but that would not show at this scale.

The waves so created are very long and very low. Their period is of the order of a thousand seconds; their wave lengths may be as much as one hundred and fifty miles; their height, only a foot or two in

deep water. The slope of the wave front is imperceptible and ships at sea are unaware of their passage.

Because the wave lengths are so long, tsunamis
move as shallow-water waves, even in the deepest
ocean. As such their velocity is controlled by the
depth.

$$C = \sqrt{gd}$$

Thus, if $g = 32$ and $d = 15,000$ feet (average
depth of the Pacific basin), the velocity of a wave in
the deep Pacific is 692 feet per second or 472 miles
an hour. Fortunately the Pacific is large enough so
that waves moving at even that speed take considerable time to cross it, and a seismic sea wave warning
system has been established to warn coastal inhabit-
ants of approaching tsunamis.

The events so far mentioned usually take place out
of sight of man where they can do little harm. It is
when these waves approach a coastline that they are
at their spectacular worst. There the influence of the
bottom topography and the configuration of the
coastline transforms the low waves of deep water
into rampaging monsters.

The first tsunami of which there is a record wiped
out Amnisos, Crete, about 1400 B.C. A thousand
years later, according to Pausanias, an ancient
Greek, "the town of Helice perished under the waters of the Gulf of Corinth where the population was
drowned to a man." In that millennium perhaps ten
tsunamis were recorded. Now two or three a year
cause local catastrophes. Certainly there is no change
in the activity of undersea earthquakes; the reason
for the apparent increase is mainly that the world's
population has grown so that people and wealth are

now spread along once deserted shores. Since this
trend is certain to continue, the danger to mankind
from great sea waves is increasing.

A list of two hundred and seventy seismic sea
waves from antiquity to 1940 was compiled by
N. H. Heck of the U. S. Coast and Geodetic Survey. In reading them one easily envisions great walls
of water suddenly towering above frantic crowds;
harbors being swept clear of ships; soaked and ter-
rorized survivors of the first wave racing the next
wave to high ground. Table V contains some choice
samples.

TABLE V
SOME GREAT SEISMIC SEA WAVES

September 14, 1509   Turkey. Sea came over the walls of
                       Constantinople and Galata following
                       earthquake.

December 16, 1575   Chile. Intense wave in the inner port
                       of Valdivia. Two Spanish galleons
                       wrecked.

March 25, 1751   Chile. City of Concepción was exten-
                       sively damaged for the fourth time
                       in a century by earthquakes. Sea
                       withdrew and returned at great
                       height several times. Disastrous ef-
                       fects at Juan Fernández Island.

November 1, 1755   Portugal. Great Lisbon earthquake.
                       Waves fifteen to forty feet high along
                       Spanish and Portuguese coasts. Very
                       high at Cádiz, where eighteen waves
                       rolled in.

December 29, 1820   Celebes, Makassar. A wall of water
                       sixty to eighty feet high swept over
                       the fort of Boelekomba. Great dam-
                       age at Nipa-Nipa and Serang-Serang.
                       A similar great wave at Bima,
                       Sumbawa, carried ships over houses.

106

August 13, 1868	South Peru (now North Chile). USS *Wateree* carried a quarter mile inshore by a wave with a maximum height of seventy feet. Receding wave uncovered Bay of Iquique to a depth of twenty-four feet and then returned with a forty-foot wave, covering the city of Iquique.
June 15, 1896	Northeast Japan. Sea waves nearly one hundred feet high at head of bay; elsewhere, ten to eighty feet. 27,000 lives lost along 320 kilometers of coast; 10,000 houses swept away.
March 16, 1926	Palmerston Island, Cook Group. Island submerged and natives lost their means of sustenance.
November 21, 1927	Chile, Aysén River region. Sea invaded land along twenty-five miles of coast. Boat *Mannesix* with crew flung into treetops of forest.
November 18, 1929	Newfoundland, Burin Peninsula. A tidal wave from the Grand Banks earthquake swept up several narrow inlets to a height of fifty feet, destroying villages and causing heavy loss.

On reading Heck's notes my first reaction was that their very terseness tended to make them more exciting than reality by stimulating the reader's imagination. However, upon examining the more extended accounts from which he took his data, I concluded that it would take a rare imagination to equal the actual circumstances. For example:

The USS *Wateree*, a Civil War side-wheeler gunboat, was stationed at Arica, Peru, in August 1868, when the tidal wave referred to by Heck occurred. According to a witness, it was "carried by an exceptionally heavy wave completely over the town, scraping the tops of the highest buildings and was safely deposited on some sandy wasteland about a mile inland. Thanks to her flat bottom she fetched up on an even keel and although it was impossible to get the ship back into her accustomed element she was in no danger structurally. The ship was therefore left in full commission for several months until sold. Service routine continued but with certain readjustments. Sanitary facilities were erected ashore and a vegetable garden was started. The most unusual modification was the substitution of burros for boats. If the captain wanted to go 'ashore,' the bosun's mate would pipe and call, 'Away brig.' Thereupon the coxswain would run out on a boom, slide down a pennant to a burro, cast off and come alongside to the ladder which had been lengthened to reach the ground. The captain would mount and ride off into the dunes."

The author well remembers how his own interest in tsunamis was generated. On April 1, 1946, our field party returned to the Berkeley campus of the University of California after five months of daily observation of the waves and beaches of the north Pacific coast and was greeted by: "Did you see the big wave?" It sounded much like an April Fool's Day joke, but, sadly, it was not. There had been a landslide in the Aleutian Trench early that morning and its waves were wreaking havoc around the Pacific basin. After the bad luck of missing the actual arrival of the waves by a day we set about collecting whatever data we could.

The next few days were spent questioning people who had seen the wave, surveying high-water marks and photographing wrecked houses and stranded boats. Some of the stories were amusing and each contained some useful fact that could be applied to the understanding of seismic sea waves. For example, we found that the first arriving crest is often so small it is unnoticed, but it is soon followed by a major recession of the water.

This happened at Half Moon Bay, where a surveying party was mapping the shoreline at the site of a proposed breakwater. The rodman's instructions were to hold the rod at the water's edge. As the water retreated with the first trough, he followed instructions. Just as the engineer on the transit was beginning to wonder how he could be reading five feet below sea level on the rod, the direction of the water movement changed; rodman and rod inadvertently surfboarded in on the first large crest.

Areas of bottom or rocks never before seen may be exposed. The first trough suddenly stranded the Half Moon Bay fishing fleet on a sandy bottom in an anchorage where it normally floated at the lowest range of the tide. But not for long. Before another ten minutes had passed the boats had refloated, dragged their anchors several hundred yards, and were stranded again—this time on a paved road thirteen feet above the original water level.

The arrival of the trough of one of these great waves should serve as a warning, but instead it attracts the curious, who often follow the receding water out to pick up flopping fish and look at the newly exposed bottom instead of running for high ground. When the next crest arrives it may come fast—in some cases it is a huge breaking wave—and the curious pay for their folly. This drop in water

109

level over a period of several minutes without change in the appearance of the usual waves is something like the rapid ebbing of the tide. In a similar way the incoming crests may be seen only as a rapid rise in the general level of the water without any observable wave front. Doubtless this tide-like action, which occurs in twelve minutes instead of twelve hours, is partly responsible for the usual misnomer "tidal wave."

On the same occasion in the cove at Pacific Grove, California, a man was dozing on a bench fifteen feet above the normal water level. He awakened when one dangling hand was wet by the gently rising water and sat bolt upright on the still-dry bench to watch the surrounding water slowly recede again. At the same instant, in nearby Monterey harbor, marine biologist Rolf Bolin noticed unusual currents around his skiff but no important rise or fall of water level.

These incidents raised an interesting question. Why should there be this major difference in the height of the wave at two points only a mile apart? Part of the answer seems to be that Pacific Grove faced away from the wave, Monterey faced into it.

Later, over a period of years, I traveled to many Pacific shores asking about the effects of that tsunami. Remarkably often points facing into the waves and bays facing away from them were hardest hit. For example, Taiohai village at the head of a narrow south-facing bay in the Marquesas Islands four thousand miles from the earthquake epicenter was demolished. Hilo, Hawaii, only half as far from the disturbance and whose offshore topography seems precisely suited to funnel tsunamis toward the town, fared worse. There the captain of a ship standing off the port watched with astonishment as the city was destroyed by waves that passed unnoticed under the ship. Another ship, the *Brigham Victory*, was unloading lumber at Hilo when the tsunami struck. The ship survived with considerable damage but the pier and its buildings were destroyed. One hundred and seventy-three persons died and $25 million in property damage was done by the waves at Hilo that morning.

But the truly great waves of April 1 struck at Scotch Cap, Alaska, only a few hundred miles from the tsunami's source, where five men were on duty in a lighthouse that marked Unimak Pass. The lighthouse building was a substantial two-story reinforced concrete structure with its foundation thirty-two feet above mean sea level. None of the men survived to tell the story but a breaking wave over one hundred feet high must have demolished the building at about 2:40 A.M. The next day Coast Guard aircraft, investigating the loss of radio contact, were astonished to discover only a trace of the lighthouse foundation. Nearby a small block of concrete one hundred and three feet above the water had been wiped clean of the radio tower it once supported.

TSUNAMI WARNING SYSTEMS

Largely as a result of the Hilo disaster a seismic sea wave warning system has been developed by the U. S. Coast and Geodetic Survey. It works like this. Ten seismograph stations around the Pacific rim from the Philippines to Alaska and from Peru to

Japan are equipped with automatic alarm systems and visible recorders. When the tremors from a large earthquake are received, the alarm sounds, alerting the local observers, who transmit the recorded data to a central station in Honolulu. If analysis there of the arrival times of the first earthquake shock at the various stations shows that the quake is located under the ocean, a radio message containing estimated times of arrival of a possible tsunami is sent to tide-measuring stations nearest the quake's epicenter. Each station is asked to report back whether or not such waves actually arrive. If unusual wave activity is reported, a warning is issued to local authorities (civil defense and police) in coastal areas that may be affected. At present no attempt is made to estimate the height of the waves to be expected, but that may be possible after further research is done.

Walter Munk was an early consultant in the development of tsunami warning devices and on passing through Hilo in 1950 could not resist the chance to ask about the workings of the embryonic system. He found the instrument was mounted at the outer end of the Hilo pier and was designed to detect waves in the one thousand second band midway between the longer period tides and the shorter period swell. The arrival of a tsunami at this finely tuned instrument would actuate an alarm bell in the police station some distance inland and the city could be warned in time to flee to higher ground.

However, the police chief, with a fine distrust of such gadgets, passed the word that no warning would be given until he telephoned a man at the end of the pier who would visually inspect the standard tide gauge and confirm the existence of unusual waves.

Aside from the obvious delay involved under the best of circumstances, this procedure seemed to place undue emphasis on the necessity for tsunamis to arrive during working hours. Even then, if the phone on the pier was not answered, a question would remain as to whether the pier, gauge, and telephone had been swept away or whether the observer was busy elsewhere. But the plan did eliminate false alarms.

After a more recent trip, several tsunamis later, Professor Munk reports an increased mutual respect between the ocean and the chief.

The need of Pacific-rim cities for a wave warning system was clear enough and over a period of years a combination of false alarms and small tsunamis made it possible to "work the bugs out of the system." When needed for one of the greatest tsunamis of the past century, it was ready.

On May 22, 1960, a violent earthquake (magnitude 8.5) shook the coast of Chile. A volcano erupted; there was widespread faulting, subsidence, and hundreds of landslides. In a local disaster area five hundred miles long, four thousand people died, half a million homes were damaged, and $400 million worth of property was destroyed. There was also a major subsidence on the great undersea fault that parallels the coast, and this generated a tsunami that was felt on all Pacific shores.

In Chile itself dozens of waterfront towns were devastated. Coastal cities in New Zealand, Australia, the Philippines, and Okinawa were flooded by several feet of water. On the U.S. coast, Los Angeles and San Diego harbors suffered a million dollars worth of damage to piers and small craft. In Japan, nine thousand miles from the origin, the waves were as much as fifteen feet high. There, 180 people died and the damage was estimated at $50 million.

But Hilo, Hawaii, again took the worst blow, and although the property damage was more serious than in 1946, this time the population was warned and there were few deaths. The sequence of events abstracted from the log of the Coast and Geodetic Survey's Honolulu observatory is an interesting record of the progress of the wave:

0938   Alarm sounded by distant earthquake.

0959   Requested data from other stations.

1014, 1120   Seismograph stations at Berkeley, Tucson, Fairbanks, Suva report in.

1059   Requested tide report from Balboa, Canal Zone.

1159   Issued bulletin (not warning) to Honolulu police and military:
This is a seismic sea wave advisory bulletin. A severe earthquake has occurred in Chile. It is possible a damaging sea wave has been generated. If so, it will reach Hawaii about midnight.

1204   Valparaiso reports tsunami on coast of Chile.

1340   Issued news bulletin reconfirming that a wave may be on the way.

1847   Issued official warning:
This is a seismic sea wave warning. The estimated time of arrival of the first wave at Hawaii is midnight. The danger may last several hours. The intensity of the wave cannot be predicted. [Arrival times estimated for Tahiti, Christmas Island, Samoa, Fiji, Canton, Johnson, Midway.]

1924   Balboa reports no wave; Christmas Island reports negative.

2223   Tahiti reports unusual wave activity [first actual tsunami report other than Chile].

2255, 0011   Samoa and La Jolla report tidal rise.

0035 Heard via broadcast band radio that unusual wave activities had begun in Hilo.

0611 All clear sounded by civil authorities.

The "unusual wave activities" that began almost exactly at midnight at Hilo included the arrival of a series of waves whose crests reached fifteen feet above the normal high water mark. As these successive walls of water swept across the city, they carried before them virtually all the buildings on seven city blocks. The record of the Hilo tide gauge (Figure 42), which went off scale and was rendered inopera-

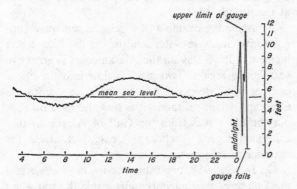

FIG. 42. Tsunami recorded on tide gauge at Hilo, Hawaii. Abruptly at midnight on May 23, 1960, a series of great seismic waves began arriving which wrecked the city. The gauge that ordinarily records tides with a four-foot range hit the stops at top and bottom before being smashed by the third wave.

ble by the second wave, shows the abruptness of the beginning of the large waves.

There is little practical action that can be taken to prevent property damage by such waves. Changing the underwater configuration or building a sufficiently large breakwater would be exceedingly expensive, but these possibilities are now being tested on models of the Hilo offshore area. Probably Hilo's best solution is to move to higher ground nearby and make the waterfront area into Tsunami Park. Doubtless this low area will be swept again and again by future waves.

The remarkable thing about the ocean is how calm and stable its surface is. Considering its breadth and depth, the changes in height caused by waves and tides are insignificant, except to those who live at the water's edge.

A fascinating example of a seismic sea wave generated by an above-water landslide is the Lituya Bay incident. Lituya Bay on the Alaska coast is an active earthquake region. Two glaciers flow into the upper end of the steep-sided bay; near its center is Cenotaph Island; a sandspit across the mouth keeps out the big waves from the Gulf of Alaska so that fishermen regard Anchorage Cove, just inside the entrance, a safe haven.

On July 9, 1958, two fishing boats, the *Badger* and the *Sunmore*, were anchored just inside the spit when a major earthquake occurred. The shock started landslides which cleaned the soil and timber off the mountainsides at the upper end of the bay at eighteen hundred feet above sea level and at the same time caused great masses of ice to fall from the front of the glaciers into the water.

An eyewitness account by the skipper of the forty-foot *Badger* gives a vivid picture of the result. He felt the earthquake, and looking inland saw the first wave building at the head of the bay. As it passed

116

Cenotaph Island he estimated its height at fifty feet (measurements made later indicated it probably was much higher). It swept through Anchorage Cove, carrying the *Badger* over the spit at an altitude of about a hundred feet and dropping it in the open sea. There the boat foundered, but the boatman was able to launch a skiff and he and his wife were picked up by another fishing boat. The fifty-five-foot *Sunmore* was not so fortunate; it was swept against a cliff and no trace of it or its crew was ever found.

This wave, although very high, was very localized. The somewhat unusual circumstance of its origin leads one to muse on the great waves that must have been generated in billions of years of geological time. One can visualize the walls of water that must have raced outward when whole mountains suddenly slid into the sea, or when a continental perimeter abruptly shifted, or when a great meteorite landed in the sea—a pebble in earth's puddle.

EXPLOSION-GENERATED WAVES

Tsunamis may also be generated by large violent explosions; fortunately such an origin is much less likely than an undersea earthquake. The classic example of an explosion-generated wave is the eruption of the volcano Krakatoa in the Sunda Straits, Dutch East Indies. This story is best told by excerpts from the words of the original report:

"Krakatoa erupted with the most violent explosions of recorded history. The entire north portion of the island was blown away and in place of ten square miles of land with an average elevation of 700 feet,

117

there was formed a great depression with its bottom more than 900 feet below sea level. Apparently pent-up superheated vapor exploded and ruptured the throat of the volcano allowing cold ocean water to "freeze" a crust on the rising molten magma there. Then, as with a safety valve tied down, the pressure began to build up. On the morning of August 27, 1883, this crust let go.

"Over four cubic miles of rock was blown away; the sea was covered with masses of pumice for miles around—in many places of such thickness that no vessel could force its way through. Two new islands rose in the strait, the lighthouses were swept away. A column of dust rose 17 miles and spread out so that at Batavia, a hundred miles away, the sky was so dark that lamps had to be burned in the houses at midday. Eventually this dust was distributed by stratospheric winds over the entire earth. The sound of the principal explosion was heard 3000 miles away and the atmospheric shock wave reflected off itself at the antipodes of the earth.

"But the most damaging effect was that of the waves which inundated the whole of the shores of Java and Sumatra which border the strait. Many villages were carried away including Tyringin and Telok Betong where the water reached heights of 60 and 72 feet. The town of Merak, at the head of a funnel-shaped bay, was struck by a wave variously estimated at 100 and 135 feet high. More than 36,000 people were drowned and many vessels were washed ashore including the man-of-war *Berouw* which was carried 1.8 miles inland and left 30 feet above sea level.

"How the wave was formed, whether by large

pieces of the island falling into the sea; by a sudden submarine explosion, by the violent movement of the crust of the earth under water; or by the sudden rush of water into the cavity of the volcano when the side was blown out, must ever remain, to a great extent, uncertain."

The waves radiated westward from the straits into the Indian Ocean, around the Cape of Good Hope, and northward through the Atlantic. Tide gauges in harbors at South Africa (4690 miles from the source), at Cape Horn (7820 miles), and Panama (11,470) clearly traced the arrivals of a series of about a dozen waves, which had traveled at an average velocity of about four hundred miles per hour. The period of the waves taken from tide stations nearby the explosion is about two hours; at great distances it is closer to one hour. No explanation can yet be given, but a similar decrease in period with distance is noted in the records of the May 1960 tsunami.

In early 1952 the author was given the job of measuring the waves from Mike, the first large thermonuclear explosion. It was to be exploded on the wide reef at the northern end of Eniwetok atoll, in the Marshall Islands. Somehow it would make waves, but by what mechanism, and how large would the waves be? The best guide was the Krakatoa report of the Royal Society of London, and I prepared an extensive abstract of it from which the preceding account has been taken. We guessed that the energy released by Mike would be about the same as that of the main explosion at Krakatoa.

Six years earlier, in the preparations for the first underwater nuclear test inside Bikini lagoon, many wave-generating experiments had been made in an attempt to forecast the size and period of the waves and the means by which they would be generated. Explosives were shot in ponds and circular steel plates were dropped into basins that contained models of the entire atoll. There was a lot of splashing and countless rolls of data were taken; there was an abundance of theories. But even after photos of the actual waves made by "Bikini Baker" had been studied, many uncertainties remained about how such waves were formed.

Mike was a different situation. It would be set off at sea level on a flat reef a mile wide. On one side was the shallow lagoon, nowhere deeper than two hundred feet. On the other side, the outer slope of the atoll dropped away into water over twelve thousand feet deep. We were nervously aware of the similarity of Krakatoa and we had to be sure that no large tsunami would be generated. If such a wave were released in deep water, it could cause damage all around the Pacific.

Mike would dig a large crater in the reef, but would it breach the outer edge of the reef? If so, the direct effect of the blast moving rock outward or the fast flow of water from the ocean back into the hole might start a wave. Experts were certain the crater would not be that large. Could the earthshock from the bomb start a landslide on the outer side of the atoll? Other experts were sure it could not because the outer slope was not quite steep enough. Could the rise in barometric pressure caused by the air shock start a wave? Yes, and although we could not estimate with certainty exactly how large it would be, we were sure that it would not be dangerous to people living around the Pacific.

The waves actually produced by Mike confirmed the advance opinions and although the hole in the reef was a mile in diameter and six hundred feet deep it did not breach the outer edge. A tsunami—a very small one—was generated. After much persuasion by me over a period of months during the preparations, a very inventive fellow named Bill Van Dorn, also of the Scripps Institution of Oceanography, consented to set up instruments and measure the characteristics of the prospective tsunami at the distant islands of Wake, Guam, and Midway.

Over a period of years Dr. Van Dorn became increasingly involved in the measurement of tsunamis and is now probably the world's expert in the field. Years later when he was selected to measure long-period waves during the International Geophysical Year, he asked that I accompany him to the islands of the South Pacific to help install wave recorders. My obligation remained so intense I could not refuse and so had to spend that year in Tahiti and the pearling islands.

WAVES PRODUCED BY SHIPS

Any disturbance of the water surface, including the passage of a ship, creates waves. But the waves made by ship are of a different kind and are studied for a different reason than we study the natural waves we have considered. Much of the power expended in propelling a ship goes into wave-making and anything that can be done to reduce these waves results in increased efficiency and is of direct economic importance. Consequently some of the greatest names of hydrodynamics are associated with the ship-wave problem, including Bernoulli, Lord Kelvin, Rankine, and the Froudes.

A ship moving through the water is accompanied by at least three pressure disturbances on each side, which produce not one but several trains of waves. In addition, the movement of the ship sets up an unusual traveling undulation that is not a wave in the ordinary sense because it stays with the ship and is nonrepeating. This undulation, sometimes visible to a practiced eye if a ship is moving at slow speed through glassy water, is called the Bernoulli contour system. It consists of two low mounds of water, one ahead of the bow, the other abaft the stern, and a broad amidships depression. This special form of a standing wave seems to be an inescapable result of ship motion if Bernoulli's theorem is satisfied.

Lord Kelvin investigated analytically the pattern of waves generated by a pressure disturbance concentrated at a point and moving in a straight line. A thin stick drawn vertically through quiet water or even a small boat on a large expanse of smooth water will create such waves. This Kelvin wave system is characterized by (1) diverging waves—a series of curved crests, concave outward and lying in echelon position; (2) transverse waves—convex forward and perpendicular to the direction of motion; (3) a line of crest intersections, where the diverging and transverse waves meet, forming a constant angle with the direction of motion. These are illustrated in Figure 43, in which the crest segments that are visible normally are indicated by heavy lines.

122

For large ships, whose hull would occupy a substantial part of the pattern just described, the mathematically ideal Kelvin system is replaced by the more realistic Velox wave system. Since various points along the hull generate waves—usually at changes in curvature along the waterline—there are usually at least four Velox systems present on each side. In fact, the wave-generating intensity is related to the abruptness of change of direction. These four gen-

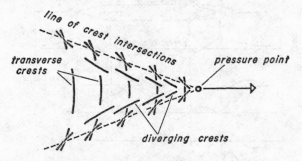

FIG. 43. Kelvin wave pattern generated by a traveling pressure point or a small boat.

erating points, shown in Figure 44, are the bow, the forward shoulder, the after shoulder, and the stern. Note that bow and stern create positive pressures and the waves begin with a crest; at the shoulders negative pressures create wave systems, beginning with a trough. When the vertical displacements of the water surface are added algebraically the answer is an approximation of the resultant wave alongside the ship. Fortunately the waves made by ship models in a towing tank are accurate predictions of those that will be created by the full-size ship they represent and check the theoretical calculations so the designer knows what a ship will do in advance of actual construction.

These various sets of waves adjust their dimensions according to ship speed and consequently interfere with each other in a complicated way. As the ship's speed increases, the waves lengthen. Of course the ship remains the same length and each wave group still originates at the same point of curvature.

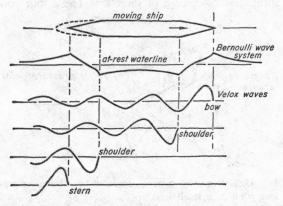

FIG. 44. Bernoulli and Velox wave systems generated by a ship and its parts. (These add in a complicated way depending on the speed of a ship.)

But now the second and third crests in each system move farther aft; at some speed these will cancel (or reinforce) the waves of the following system. Thus the pattern of waves made by a ship changes as its speed changes.

A slightly submerged streamlined body such as a submarine at periscope depth also generates surface waves. It creates a Bernoulli system and transverse Velox waves above its bow, midships, and stern points. Thus even a submarine, if it is moving at a shallow depth, spends some of its power in making waves.

Ships also may generate unseen internal waves on the interface between two layers of water of different density. In regions of rapidly melting ice or near the mouths of large rivers, a layer of fresh water often rests on the heavier oceanic salt water with little or no mixing. When this layering happens the progress of slow-moving ships is retarded because most of their propulsive energy goes into generating waves on the boundary between the fresh and salt water. These subsurface waves may be much higher and move much slower than the visible surface waves generated at the same time.

This phenomenon is known as the "Hall effect" after two brothers who studied it intensively in an

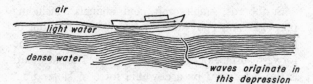

air
light water
dense water
waves originate in this depression

Fig. 45. The Hall effect. Slow-moving small craft generates waves on the interface between fresh and salt water.

Edinburgh wave tank in 1830. Much later V. W. Eckman, investigating strange tales of Norwegian fishermen who claimed their boats got "stuck" in the "dead water" of fjords, gave the following explanation:

The deep and still salt water of the fjord is "flooded" with fresh water. The bow of a fishing boat moving in the lighter-density upper layer causes a rise in pressure that depresses the fresh-salt interface just as though a thin flexible membrane separated the two. This sets a train of waves in motion on the surface of the salt water which move at about one eighth the speed of those on an air-water interface. These waves in effect "capture" the boat that creates them so that waves and boat move together as a unit. Then the resistance of the slow-interval waves adds to that of the ship. This is the reason why, once a ship is slowed-down and caught in the position shown in Figure 45, escape is difficult. Eckman suggested that fishing craft could avoid this difficulty by maintaining a speed above five knots.

SURFING ON WAVES

Surfboards, small craft, and animals (including porpoises and body-surfers) can take energy out of the waves to propel themselves by sliding down the forward surface of an advancing wave. The surfboard is thrust forward by a downhill force or slope drag, shown in Figure 46 as a vector connecting the gravity force to the buoyancy force (which always acts perpendicular to the water surface). When the slope drag is greater than the hydrodynamic drag (water resistance) the object moves at wave-crest speed. The trick of surfing, of course, is to get the board moving and the weight properly balanced so that the slope drag can take over the work of propulsion at the moment the wave passes beneath. If the surfboard is also moving sidewise across the face of the wave, it may move at a considerably higher velocity than the wave itself.

Dukws—amphibious trucks used for surveying the surf zone—not only can assume the proper slope, but also can take advantage of an additional effect to "surfboard" on large breaking waves. Their front axles hang down so as to offer a vertical surface for

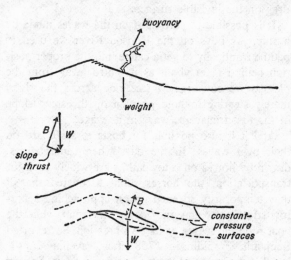

FIG. 46. Slope thrust drives the surfer and the porpoise. (after Harold Saunders)

the orbiting water particles to press against. Body-surfers who hold their hands down beneath their bodies can get the same kind of boost.

The air-water interface is a surface of constant pressure; beneath it are other parallel surfaces of constant pressure that move with imaginary waves that are subsurface reflections of the visible waves above.

Porpoises are neutrally buoyant and with a little

practice learn to tilt themselves at the proper slope to take advantage of the slope drag to surfboard on some underwater constant-pressure surface. These animals can ride beneath the bow wave of a ship indefinitely without appearing to exert any effort at all. Apparently a porpoise can do this because the skin drag of his curious hide is less than the slope drag on the invisible surface.

It is possible to surfboard on the waves made by a ship. As boys on the Hudson River we used to paddle frantically to get a canoe into the proper position behind a ferryboat as it pulled away from the pier so we could get a free ride across the river, merely steering to hold position on the steep slope of the first transverse wave in its wake.

And it is also possible for boats to surfboard on their own waves. In the days when canal barges, drawn by horses on a towpath, were widely used for transportation, the horses soon discovered that if they temporarily speeded up on approaching a narrow stretch of canal, they could then relax while the boat rode the waves of its own creation. So reported Benjamin Franklin in 1768 after traveling on the canals of France. Many years later Scott Russell studied "fly boats" on the Scottish canals where the same "advantageous principle was employed to reach high speeds in the passenger trade."

The canals were very shallow (probably less than four feet) so that the waves moved at $\sqrt{gd}$ velocity or about ten feet a second (7 mph). One can imagine that when the canal suddenly narrowed and the height of the bow wave increased, a wise horse (or driver) would smile to himself at the prospect of surfboarding his load for a while.

In 1946 an interesting accident to an integrated barge flotilla on the Mississippi River reminded modern barge operators of the importance of these waves. This flotilla was made of eleven sections twelve hundred feet long pushed by the towboat *Harry Truman*. On one occasion, after many successful trips, the bow unit (one hundred feet long and fifty-four-foot beam) suddenly jackknifed and lifted twelve feet out of the water, breaking up the flotilla. It was apparent that the bow had not hit bottom and investigation subsequently showed that the bow had passed over a shoal that had caused the bow wave to peak up abruptly. So a ship (or at least a train of barges) can destroy itself with its own waves.

Chapter VII

MEASURING WAVES AND
MAKING WAVES

Scientific progress is largely dependent on the ability to make better measurements. Therefore much wave research of recent years has been directed towards the development of new kinds of instruments and techniques for measuring waves. The understanding of how and why measurements are made as they are gives one a much better insight into the nature of wave motion.

Until the early 1940s direct observation, the photograph, and the tide gauge were the principal means available for studying waves. The observer would watch the sea surface and make notes. He would record the number of seconds between wave crests passing a piling (or the bow of his ship) and estimate the height of each one. This was not very satisfactory at night or when the ship was moving; besides, with this method, the sea has to be watched constantly or unusual events will be missed. Moreover, the dynamic quality is lost in a series of uncertain tabulations: wave crests cross each other; secondary crests ride on the flanks of large waves; the crests a little way off are aligned with the trough being observed. Except near the shore, where the effect of the bottom tends to "organize" the waves, a

thoroughly confusing situation exists, too complicated to be retained or analyzed by the human mind.
Only a general impression could be obtained. Clearly,
measuring and recording instruments were needed.

WAVE OBSERVATIONS

The first step was to stop the motion and "freeze"
the shape of the sea surface by photographing it.
Then the instantaneous situation could be studied
at leisure. From single still-photos the photographic
technique evolved to stereo-pairs taken from a ship's
mast so that wave height could be obtained and the
sea surface contoured. Then came motion pictures of
waves under many conditions—at sea in storms,
breaking waves on the beach, slow-motion movies
of waves in tanks, and fast-motion (time-lapse)
movies of waves in harbors. Sometimes, in order to
give scale to the photograph, markers were introduced; these included floating disks and spar buoys
graduated in feet. A spar buoy is a slender buoyant
pipe that floats vertically; often it is attached by a
rubber cord to a horizontal damping disk that hangs
far beneath. This reduces its vertical motion to a
minimum as the waves pass.

Aerial photography for wave research explored a
whole series of possibilities. By analysis of precisely
timed wave photographs, techniques were developed
for measuring the depth of water in the approaches
to an enemy-held beach. The Waves Project field
party made radio-controlled photo sequences in
which pictures of the surf zone were taken simultaneously from an aircraft at twelve thousand feet, the

131

top of a cliff and the beach. From analysis of these pictures it was possible to determine what waves were arriving and how they were affected by the underwater contours. Walter Munk used the "Cox lens" (lens removed from camera) to record the sun's glitter pattern on the sea surface and determine the average slope of the waves and the power spectrum of the sea under various wind conditions.

In addition to the photographic methods of measuring and recording ocean waves, sound beams and radio beams also have been tried. Aircraft in level flight at low altitude above the water can use a recording radio altimeter to get wave height. Submarines can point an echo sounder upward and record changes in the distance to the water surface above as waves pass. Or, in shallow water, a recording echo-sounder in a small boat that is hove-to will give an approximate picture of the waves that raise and lower the boat relative to the bottom. Most of these were tools rather than instruments; they made wave observations more convenient and reduced the demands on estimation and memory. But a true instrument does something more. It amplifies sensory perception and makes it possible to learn things that could never be discovered by the ordinary human senses. Most of the present instrumentation had its beginnings in the later days of World War II, when research was driven by the expected need to forecast or otherwise determine wave conditions on enemy-held beaches where amphibious landings might have to be made.

The development of an instrument begins with an analysis of the properties of the subject. What qualities of waves can be sensed and measured?

Table VI summarizes wave properties and lists instruments that have been used most generally. Although there are quite a few, the list is by no means complete and perhaps the reader will be able to think of still other means of measuring waves. More than likely he will reinvent some previously tried instrument, for by now virtually every possibility seems to have been explored. Somehow the existence of many varieties of instruments, instead of satisfying the demand, seemingly has challenged wave investigators to devise new forms that employ different principles.

Mrs. Kaye Steele accepted the challenge and invented a device that would make use of parrots for transducers, and would sense the wetting property of waves. The parrots are spaced at one-foot vertical intervals so that as the wave passes the wetting effect of the wave is transformed by the parrot into sound energy in the form of a loud squawk. The scientist (on shore) is only to count the squawks to learn the height of the wave. Mrs. Steele's ingenuity seems to have laid the conceptual groundwork for the step resistance gauge of the U. S. Corps of Engineers, which came later.

This is not the place for any detailed description of wave-measuring devices, but it seems worthwhile to describe a few of the major forms of instruments that have contributed substantially to modern wave theory.

TIDE GAUGES

The oldest instrument is the tide gauge, invented by Lord Kelvin in 1882 and brought to a high de-

TABLE VI

INSTRUMENTS FOR MEASURING WAVES

Property to be sensed	Means of sensing	How used
Light reflection	Visual	Too many ways to enumerate here
	Camera	
Height of water surface	Float in pipe	Standard tide gauge
	Spar buoy	In deep water with deep damping disk
	Aneroid barometer	Measures heave of ship
	Radio waves	Radio altimeter on low-flying aircraft
	Echo sounder	Pointed down from buoy in shallow water or up from submarine in deep water
	Step gauge	Water closes contacts between spark plugs
	Paired wires	For model tank experiments with very small waves

Pressure at sea floor	Flexible bellows plus:	
	Bourdon tube	Uncoiling tube drives pen
	Potentiometer	Bridge circuit to galvanometer
	Variable inductance	Measures change in magnetic field
	Thermopile	Measures adiabatic heating of air
	Strain gauge	Measures change in length of metal
	Air bladder	Directly drives pen via air hose to surface
	Vibrator	Changes frequency as pressure changes
Water motion (velocity or acceleration)	Accelerometer	Mounted on buoy to measure acceleration of waves
	Accelerometer-pressure comb.	Shipboard wave recorder that computes wave height for several sensors
	Rotor	Measures currents caused by waves
Drag	Strain gauge	Senses wave forces acting on special pile
Direction	Rayleigh disk	Orients itself parallel to wave front
Impact	Dynamometer	Sliding bar moves to show maximum force
	Diaphragm	Same as above plus hydrostatic force
	Piezoelectric disks	Electronic amplification of force

gree of reliability by the U. S. Coast and Geodetic
Survey. It is usually set up on a pier in the quiet
waters of a harbor or protected bay—not in the open
ocean. A pipe, perhaps a foot in diameter, open at
both top and bottom extends from near the harbor
floor to well above the highest tide level. Inside the

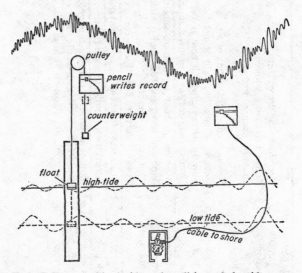

FIG. 47. Record of both tide and swell is made by tide gauge
(pipe open at bottom) or by absolute pressure transducer,
which measures the pressure of *A* relative to *B*.

pipe (sometimes called a stilling well) is a float; from
the top of the float a wire extends up around a drive
shaft and down to a counterweight. A clockwork
mechanism keeps chart paper moving slowly beneath
the drive shaft and attached to the latter on a lead
screw is a pencil. As the tide—and the float—rises and

falls, the pencil position moves back and forth, tracing out the height of the water on the paper.

When Lord Kelvin, who is best known for his abstract formulation of the second law of thermodynamics, presented his scientific findings with this instrument to the Institute of Civil Engineers, he was roundly criticized for having used a pencil instead of a fountain pen (which had just been invented). In answering the derogatory comments Kelvin said, in part, ". . . the ink marker has been tried for tide gauges and has hitherto been found unsuccessful on account of the slowness of the motion, but there is ample power in the tide gauge to drive a pencil." He further remarked, ". . . good workmanship is too often required to overcome the evils of a poor design."

Professor Carl Eckart of Scripps thinks that these wise words should be called Kelvin's First and Second Laws of Oceanographic Instrumentation: (1) "There is ample driving power in the sea"; (2) The instrument should not depend on precision parts for its operation.

Tide gauges are usually set up in the quiet waters of a harbor, where they are not exposed to any swell and their pipes extend deep enough so that the small waves generated inside the harbor do not affect the float. If the same device were attached to a pier extending out into the ocean, the float would rise and fall with each passing swell. This is because the open lower end of the pipe would permit the water to flow in and out rapidly and the water surface inside would be at the same level as that outside.

However, a small change in the instrument con-

verts it into a long-period wave recorder. If the bottom end of the pipe were completely sealed off, the
water level inside would not change. But if this seal
has a small hole in it, the pressure created by the

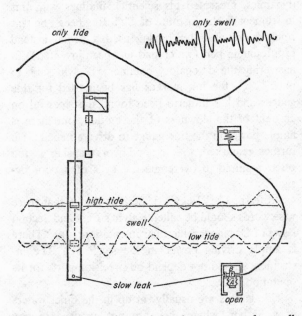

FIG. 48. Tide-gauge pipe, sealed at bottom except for small
hole which lets water leak slowly in and out, draws smooth
record of the tide. Differential pressure transducer measures
pressure at *A* relative to that at *B*. The small tube allows water to leak slowly in and out of chamber *B* so that only swell
is recorded.

passage of a wave crest will cause water to flow
through the hole and raise the level inside the pipe
slightly. Short-period waves and even ocean swell
go by too quickly to permit enough water to flow

through the hole to appreciably change the water level in the pipe. But long waves with periods of several minutes maintain the pressure long enough for the water level inside to respond. Therefore, even though these waves are only a few inches high in the midst of a turbulent zone of waves five feet or more in height, this instrument measures only the low long-period waves and ignores the much higher swell.

The hole restricts the flow to a slow leak and its size can be computed to "tune" the instrument to the desired period. Such is the principle of Walter Munk's long-period (tsunami) recorder on Scripps pier which first recorded surf beat.

WAVE RECORDERS

In the late 1940s the author headed a field party of the Waves Project of the University of California that installed twenty or thirty wave recorders off the California, Oregon, and Washington coasts, usually just outside the surf zone. These operated on various principles as we experimented with one scheme and then another to find the best way of measuring the deep-sea swell. Some operated for several years; others were knocked out in a few hours—the Pacific Ocean is a tough proving ground. But we did get results, and the effort produced miles of chart paper covered with good records of waves, enough to form a sound basis for the first statistical summary of Pacific swell.

These measuring-recording systems were generally similar. A differential pressure pickup on a steel tripod rested on the sea floor in thirty to sixty feet of water; an armored submarine cable encasing three or four electrical conductors led ashore to a recorder in a shack on the beach. As the waves passed over, the sensor detected the changes in pressure at the bottom caused by the differences in the height of water above the instrument. The signals were elec-

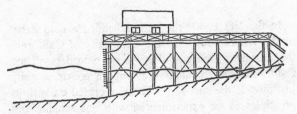

FIG. 49. Shore-based wave recorders. *Top:* Pressure-sensing pickup mounted in tripod on ocean floor. *Bottom:* Step-resistance wave meter mounted on pier.

trically transmitted ashore, and on a moving chart a pen traced a red line representing the crests and troughs of the passing waves.

In most cases the transducer, a device that changes pressure into an electrical signal, was actuated by the motion of a bellows. (A bellows is a small metal cylinder with corrugated sides that can expand and contract as the pressure changes.)

In the tsunami recorder described earlier the problem was to get rid of the effect of swell and record only long-period waves. But in these recorders we wanted to look only at the swell and eliminate the effect of the long-period waves and tides.

An absolute or total pressure recorder would measure all waves (including swell and tides), superimposed one on another, plus the weight of the water above the instrument and the atmospheric pressure. Obviously the chart required to record eight-foot waves atop an eight-foot tide is twice as wide as that required for the wave alone. Moreover, it is more convenient to analyze a wave record that is made relative to the straight line of instantaneous sea level than relative to the changing curve of the tide. So the differential pressure sensor is designed to remove the effect of the tide.

The differential pressure instrument measures the rapidly changing pressure of the passing wave relative to the slowly changing pressure of the average sea level. In the long-period wave recorder the water level inside the pipe remained almost at average sea level, moving only slightly up and down in response to waves with a three-minute period. This relative stability was attained by allowing the water outside the pipe to leak in and out slowly through a small hole. The swell recorder makes use of the same technique to obtain a reference pressure. In it the instantaneously changing pressure in A caused by the waves with period of up to twenty seconds flexes the bellows in and out. Chamber B is sealed except for a very small hole so that it maintains a reference

141

pressure equivalent to that of average sea-level at
the moment. Then the transducer T measures the
instantaneous wave pressure in the bellows A relative
to average sea level pressure.

Most subsurface wave-measuring instruments work
in a similar manner; the differences usually are in the
kinds of pressure transducer used.

The bottom-mounted wave-pressure recorder has
both advantages and disadvantages. Since it is installed usually in water thirty or more feet deep, the
higher frequency waves are filtered out by the depth
and do not confuse the record. That is, chop and
small wind waves do not affect the pressure pickup
on the bottom (because it is deeper than half their
wave length). This is a disadvantage only to those
who are interested in the small waves.

The bottom recorder requires no special installation offshore and can be placed almost anywhere on
the bottom. On the other hand, it is harder to service and may be covered with sand in some seasons
and thus rendered inoperable.

A pressure record is not a precise reflection of
the sea surface. It ignores the small waves, and the
indicated heights of large waves must be modified
according to the calibration curve of the instrument.

In order to overcome these objections the Beach
Erosion Board of the Corps of Engineers developed
a step-resistance wave gauge. The gauge consists of a
pipe twenty-five feet long mounted vertically on one
piling of a pier so that its midpoint is about at mean
sea level. At intervals of 0.2 of a foot along its length,
pairs of contact points (modified spark plugs) project from the pipe. As the crest of a wave approaches,
the salt water closes the circuit across the spark plug

gaps; as it passes, the contacts are broken. Resistors in the circuit are so selected that when power is applied the variation in current flow is proportional to submerged length of pipe.

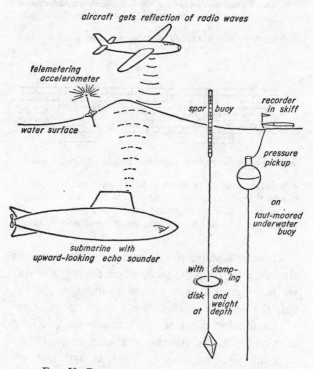

aircraft gets reflection of radio waves

telemetering accelerometer

water surface

spar buoy

recorder in skiff

pressure pickup

on taut-moored underwater buoy

submarine with upward-looking echo sounder

with damping

disk and weight at depth

FIG. 50. Deep-water wave-measuring methods.

A record of the electric current flowing then becomes a direct record of the history of the height of the sea surface alongside the pier. Chop, wind waves, swell and tides, each atop the others, are all recorded simultaneously in magnificent confusion.

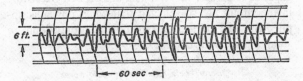

bottom-pressure record (water 40 feet deep)

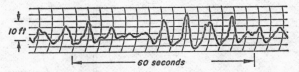

step-resistance record (surface height alongside pier)

Fig. 51. Recordings of waves in which wave height is plotted against time. Note that the record of bottom-pressure changes caused by swell is nearly sinusoidal whereas that of the wave surface (in a storm) shows long troughs and pointed crests.

There is also interest in measuring the waves in the ocean far from the shore where the depth of water is so great that a bottom recorder would see only the very long waves. It is possible to make use of this filtering effect of depth selectively to record tides and tsunamis. Another possibility once tried by the author is to mount a shallow-water type pressure recorder on top of a submerged buoy that is held about a hundred feet below the surface by a taut wire anchored to the bottom.

A more commonly used method of measuring waves in deep water is to mount an accelerometer in a floating buoy and directly record the acceleration of the buoy caused by the passing waves. One version of this developed by the Navy is the Splashnik, which is intended to be expendable but has the disadvantage that the users often spend a good deal of time trying to retrieve it. Another accelerometer system has been developed by M. J. Tucker, of the British National Institute of Oceanography, into what is perhaps the most sophisticated instrument of all: the shipboard wave recorder.

The ship takes the place of the buoy, but because a ship is large compared to the waves, a combination of accelerometers and pressure pickups at the bow and stern is required. The instruments are mounted in the hull about ten feet below the normal water level. The pressure sensor measures the height of passing waves above this point, and the accelerometer measures the height of the pressure pickup relative to average sea level. The signals are fed into a central computer which sorts out the data and records the major waves.

No wave-direction recorder has ever worked very well, the reason apparently being that waves from so many directions are always present and the direction sensor is as confused as any human observer would be. There certainly ought to be a handsome reward offered to the inventor of a good one. So far, the most practicable direction sensor was devised by John Isaacs in 1949 and placed by the author a half mile off Point Arguello, the most exposed point on the Southern California coast. His direction sensor was a Rayleigh disk about a foot in diameter which has the property that it always orients itself perpendicular to the water motion (in contrast to a wind vane which stays parallel to the motion). This technique was used because the wave orbital currents change direction by 180° as a wave passes and a disk does not have to flip from side to side as a vane would. It was mounted on a tripod on the sea floor in about forty feet of water, alongside a wave-pressure sensor. A submarine cable brought the electrical signals from the two instruments ashore, where they were recorded on the same chart. The idea was to detect the direction from which the large waves and trains of waves were coming, at least to the nearest compass point. We hoped to be able to track shifting storm centers or at least to determine if the swell was coming from the Southern Hemisphere. Sometimes it seemed to work well; other times we were not so sure. Certainly the relationship between the pressure records and the current at the sea floor was more complex than we had expected.

Wave Force Measurement

Another class of instrument makes it possible to measure the force exerted by waves on pilings, piers, and shoreline structures. Some instruments have been used to observe storm wave forces and obtain data that can be applied in the design of future offshore structures, such as Texas towers (for oil drilling). Others are intended to determine the shock caused by the impact of a breaking wave on a breakwater or other very shallow water structure.

The measurement of wave forces on pilings is complicated by the continual reversal of direction of the water as the crest moves in one direction and the trough moves in the other. The water velocities in the various parts of the wave vary with time and with depth. Moreover, since the force is caused by the rush of water past the pile (the drag), the answer is sensitive to the square of the velocity as well as to the shape and size of the piling. There are so many unknown factors that Jack Morrison, of the Waves Project group, decided that it would be best to determine the answers directly by experiment, first in the model tank, then in the field. In the test, especially instrumented pile sections were exposed to ocean waves under various sets of conditions.

As shown in Table VII the forces imposed on pilings by swell are relatively modest, but as the wave begins to break and the water particle velocity increases, waves of about the same period and height cause substantially greater forces. One moral of this story is: when possible, build your structure in water too deep to cause waves to break.

Most Texas towers are built in sufficiently deep water to avoid shoaling breakers, but when great hurricanes sweep across the Gulf, the towers must withstand breaking waves at sea. Oil company engineers have made similar measurements on the towers during such storms and obtained data roughly equivalent to that given here.

The Corps of Engineers, which is responsible for the maintenance of harbors and coastal structures, is especially interested in the large instantaneous pressures created by the impact of water moving at high velocity in breakers. Over a period of years, it has conducted experiments to determine how great these

147

TABLE VII
WAVE FORCES ON PILING

Wave type	Wave period (seconds)	Wave height (feet)	Measured force (pounds)	Total moment (ft. lbs.)	Drag Coefficient
Swell	9.3	3.4	9	85	.32
Peaked-up swell	10.0	3.1	10	93	.49
Wave immediately before breaking	10.8	3.3	19	186	.86
Breaker	10.3	3.3	23	226	1.28
Foamline (wave of translation)	10.3	3.5	33	320	1.46

These data for waves of similar height and period were obtained with a 3.5-inch-diameter test piling ten feet long at Monterey, California, in 1953. Notice the substantial increase in force on the piling as waves change from swell into breakers and then foamlines.

shock pressures can be and how new structures might be designed to resist them. Anyone who has stood on a rocky coast in a storm has felt the ground shake under the waves and seen the water hurled high into the air, and will have some appreciation of the problem. The pressure required to project water into the air is about one half a pound per square inch for each foot of height. Thus, water going forty feet into the air requires twenty psi or an impact load of nearly a ton and a half on each square foot of rock.

The shock-pressure gauge consists of a stack of thin plates of tourmaline crystal set in a strong metal case. When subjected to pressure, this gauge produces a small charge of electricity which can be amplified, measured with an oscilloscope, and recorded with a camera. In wave-channel experiments, waves only six inches high have produced pressures as high as eighteen psi—but lasting only a thousandth of a second.

MAKING WAVES

In an early chapter the simplest and most widely used form of wave channel was described. A paddle-type generator made waves in the simple sine pattern on which wave theory rests. There are many other kinds of wave-makers, however, and many other uses for model waves in controlled conditions. Experimental facilities range in size from tabletop ripple tanks to maneuvering basins much larger than a football field.

Why make experimental waves? There are many reasons, beginning with scientific curiosity about the nature of waves themselves. Better answers are needed to the questions: How are waves created? What shape are the orbits under various conditions? How are they propagated? What are the conditions under which waves of different sizes refract, reflect, diffract?

The shoreline engineer must know in advance of construction the effects of various kinds and sizes of waves on beaches, breakwaters, groins, jetties, seawalls, and similar structures. How effective will these structures be in protecting a harbor or stopping the drift of sand along the coast? How high should a new dam be to prevent storm waves from going over the top? What size rocks should be used in the breakwater?

The naval architect wants to tow ship models in wave conditions simulating a true seaway and determine the magnitude of the stresses in each hull. He can discover also how seaworthy a design will be and can estimate the speed that some future ship will be able to make into the teeth of a gale that will blow a dozen years hence.

Each of these areas of interest may require a special wave tank to duplicate properly the shape and motion of the natural water surface. Let us begin with the very shallow, glass-bottomed ripple tank used both for teaching students about waves of all kinds (including sound and light) and for simple model studies of harbors. Often these tanks are about four feet square and a few inches deep. A bright light, shining upward from beneath, projects images of the waves onto a screen above. The wave crests produce bright images because they act as converging lenses to concentrate the light; the troughs act as diverging lenses and appear dark. These patterns of light dance on the screen, responding within a second or two to changes in the tank. It is a very convenient arrangement, and with water less than an inch deep, waves can be generated by very small motions such as dipping a finger into the tank or, more systematically, driving an elongated paddle with a simple sine-wave generator. The characteristics of wave motion can be observed and simple experiments conducted. Even this modest equipment can be of help to the harbor designer, who can use rows of dominoes to model possible breakwater arrangements and watch the effect of any change as he makes it.

The four types of wave-makers in general use are shown diagrammatically in Figure 52. Actually no particular ingenuity is required to produce waves in a tank; in fact, it would be a much more remarkable feat to do anything to the water without making waves. Each type has advantages for special applications. The paddle, the plunger, and the piston are all connected by a rigid arm to an eccentrically-located pin on a turning wheel and thus directly produce mathematically-satisfying sine waves. One can see by inspection of the diagrams how these work. It is evident that reducing the speed of the driving wheel lengthens the wave period and increasing the radius of the pin connection increases wave height. These are commonly used in long narrow wave channels to produce a large variety of wave sizes.

Pneumatic wave-makers are a more recent development; usually several of them are mounted side by side along two walls of large square tanks. They create waves by changing the air pressure beneath a hood so that the water surface there rises and falls. As the water surface inside the hood is depressed the pressure is transmitted, by Pascal's law, to the water immediately on the other side of the partition where the surface is raised. This disturbance will then travel the length of the tank. The speed of the blower

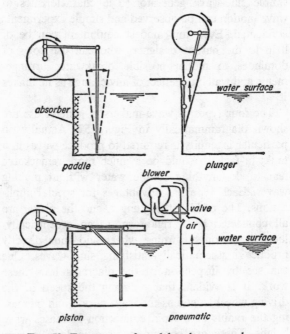

FIG. 52. Four types of model-tank wave-makers.

motor controls the amount of air pressure and thus the amplitude of the waves; the speed of the valve-operating motor controls duration of pressure and thus the wave length.

Of the many other possible ways to make waves, one of the most imaginative was invented by W. G. Van Dorn who wanted to create very long, very low tsunami-like waves in a small tank. His apparatus is a channel about a foot wide, a few inches deep and one hundred feet long, so constructed that the bottom of the tank can be flexed by a series of motors which raise and lower the entire channel a few tenths of an inch in an undulating motion, generating micro-tsunamis as required. John Isaacs solved the tsunami-modeling problem in a different way by floating a light liquid on a denser one and making waves on the interface between the two. Such waves travel very slowly because of the small density difference. These are clever but bizarre experiments. Most of today's researchers are interested in directly duplicating a stormy ocean surface where the waves are casually described as confused. An understatement!

First it is necessary to find out what the surface is like by directly measuring the waves with a shipborne or other kind of wave meter. If the actual shape of the waves—also referred to as the "time-history of the height of the surface at a point"—is recorded on magnetic tape, it can be played back as often as desired. The next step is to devise a mechanism on which the tape recording can be played back —much as a tape of music would be played—except in this case it is reproduced on a wave-maker instead of a hi-fi set. If the height of the water at intervals of 0.1 second is scanned from the tape and fed into a wave generator at the head of a channel, the waves created are almost exactly like the ones experienced and recorded by the ship, and ship models can be towed on a realistic sea surface. The narrow channel with its two-dimensional roughness did not, however, create sufficient confusion to satisfy some scientists, and basins have been built in Holland, France, and the United States with wave generators lining two sides of the tank, each producing different waves. With these, shorelines can be subjected to complex waves, and model ships can be towed at various angles to the seaway.

Another form of wave machine is in some ways even more realistic. If the wave channel or ripple tank is covered with a low hood and air is sucked through the space above the water surface, model wind waves are created. Such an arrangement is fine for studying the mechanisms by which the wind raises waves, but it is of little use for most problems.

Most wave channels require "beaches" or wave absorbers to prevent reflections from the end opposite the wave-maker. In some cases these may actually be made of sand, but for ship-towing tanks there are more practical solutions. Many substances and surfaces have been tried, including metallic honeycomb, expanded metal, and meshes of various kinds. A gently inclined wooden beach with crosswise slots is often most satisfactory. The water runs up it and falls through the slots so that no reflection is possible.

With a choice of wave-makers that can duplicate natural waves in the ocean, the experimenter can select a tank shape that is suited to his problem and equip it to make waves of the complexity he desires. Tank shapes fall into several major classifications, each suited to a particular kind of model work. The long narrow channel is usually selected for experiments on the waves themselves, on ship models towed parallel to wave direction, for beach experiments in which the offshore-onshore motion of sand is under study, and for tests of breakwater sections. The large nearly square basins that are only a foot or two deep are generally favored for studies of the longshore transport of sand and for models of harbors. Large deep tanks are used for the maneuvering of "free" (radio-controlled) models as well as for towing large ship models at an angle to complex seas. The following descriptions of some of the largest and most elaborate wave tanks indicate how important this kind of research tool is to engineers and scientists working with oceanic problems.

E. V. Lewis of the Experimental Towing Tank at Stevens Institute of Technology seems to have been the first naval architect to inject planned realism into ship-model testing. On the assumption that a seaway never repeats itself, it is only necessary to re-create the statistical properties in order to reproduce any sea state. Since the sea surface is made up of an infinite number of sine waves randomly combined, it is possible to duplicate the surface by randomly programming the stroke of the wave-maker. On testing model ships in such waves it was discovered that the longitudinal bending moments on the ship's structure were greatly increased over the results from the regular waves previously used.

A year or so later, the ship-towing tank at the University of California at Berkeley (200 × 8 × 6 feet) was equipped with an even more ambitious irregular wave generator by Robert Wiegel and his associates. Their computer takes data from wave records and feeds it to a mechanical device that moves a piston-type or "bulkhead" generator to reproduce the sea surface originally recorded.

The Neyrpic laboratory in Grenoble, France, has developed the "snake type" wave-maker for the generation of complex seas. It is composed of a large number of small paddle-type generators side by side which can be oriented independently and operated. The line of generators is something like a vertical venetian blind and can be arranged in curves of various shapes (hence the name) to produce waves of nearly any complexity.

The Beach Erosion Board in Washington, D. C., has two outdoor tanks. One is broad and shallow (300 × 150 × 3 feet) and has ten portable wavemakers, which can be arranged in any desired fashion. These create what is happily called "short-crested confusion." There less attention is paid to precise wave generation; instead, the experimenters, using probes, directly measure the waves that actually arrive at the beach or jetty and from the data determine the significant height of the attacking waves. The other test facility is a huge wave channel 630 feet long and 20 feet square with a 500-horsepower wave generator. It can subject quarter-scale models of ocean breakwater to six-foot breakers.

The largest and most modern facilities are those at the Navy's David Taylor Model Basin in Washington, where channels and tanks permit hydrodynamic measurements of all sorts. Two of these facilities are worth special mention. The "deep water basin" is 2775 feet long, 51 feet wide and 22 feet deep. Its pneumatic wave-maker makes waves up to two feet high of any desired length. Ship models thirty-two feet long and weighing up to five tons can be towed at speeds up to sixty knots by a carriage running on heavy steel rails. These precise rails vary in height no more than two thousandths of an inch and actually take into account the curvature of the earth.

The new maneuvering and seakeeping basin, named after Captain Harold Saunders who conceived it, is 360 by 240 feet and 20 to 35 feet deep. It is spanned by a 230-ton bridge, which supports a towing carriage and can be pivoted to tow the ship models at any angle relative to the wave system. Batteries of pneumatic wave-makers along two sides can create waves up to two feet high, five to forty feet long in accordance with taped instructions. When the water surface is still and the wave-makers along one side of it are started, the phenomena of the disappearance of the first wave (mentioned in Chapter III) can be seen clearly. For some wave periods the first seven waves will disappear before a disturbance reaches the opposite end of the tank. In order to make certain that the waves in this huge tank would be satisfactory a tenth-scale model (itself bigger than many experimental basins) was built, and Wilbur Marks practiced making waves for a year or more in advance of the construction of the main tank.

With such facilities it is almost fair to say that ocean waves have been brought indoors for study.

Chapter VIII

THE SURF

Waves have many stages in their lives. They are born as ripples, grow into whitecaps, chop, wind waves, and finally into fully-developed storm seas. As these seas pass out from under the winds that formed them, they diminish in height and steepness into low sine-shaped swell. As swell, waves may traverse great stretches of open ocean without much loss of energy. Eventually they reach the shoaling waters of a continental shelf. Once on the shelf the wave fronts are bent until they almost parallel the shoreline.

All this seems to be merely preparation for the final and most exciting step. The irregular waves of deep water are organized by the effect of the bottom into long regular lines of crests moving in the same direction at similar velocities. The romanticist thinks of the forces of the sea being marshaled for an exuberant death against an ancient enemy. The depth continues to decrease until finally in very shallow water it becomes impossible for the oscillating water particles to complete their orbits. When the orbits break the wave breaks. The crest tumbles forward, falling into the trough ahead as a mass of foaming white water. The momentum carries the broken water onward until the wave's last remaining energy is expended in a gentle swash that rushes up the sandy beach face and sinks from sight. The wave is gone!

This zone where waves give up their energy and where systematic water motions give way to violent turbulence is the surf. It is the most exciting part of the ocean.

BREAKING WAVES

As the swell from the deep sea moves into very shallow water, it is traveling at a speed of fifteen to twenty miles an hour, and the changes in its character over the final few dozen yards to shore come very rapidly.

In the approach to shore the drag of the bottom causes the wave velocity to decrease. The decrease causes the phenomenon of refraction, which was described earlier, and one of its effects is to shorten the wave length. As length decreases, wave steepness increases, tending to make the waves less stable. Moreover, as a wave crest moves into water whose depth is about twice the wave height, another effect is observed which further increases wave steepness. The crest "peaks up." That is, the rounded crest that is identified with swell is transformed into a higher, more pointed mass of water with steeper flanks. As the depth of water continues to decrease, the circular orbits are squeezed into a tilted ellipse and the orbital velocity at the crest increases with the increasing wave height.

This sequence of changes in wave length and steepness is the prelude to breaking. Finally, at a depth

159

of water roughly equal to 1.3 times the wave height, the wave becomes unstable. This happens when not enough water is available in the shallow water ahead to fill in the crest and complete a symmetrical wave form. The top of the onrushing crest becomes unsupported and it collapses, falling in uncompleted orbits. The wave has broken; the result is surf.

FIG. 53. The breaking of a wave: 1. Swell peaks up on entering very shallow water. 2. At depth equal to 1.3 times the wave height, it breaks. 3. Wave re-forms and breaks again. 4. Water moves beachward as wave of translation. 5. Finally rushes up the beach.

Having broken into a mass of turbulent tumbling foam, carried landward by its own momentum, the ex-wave will, if the water deepens again as it does after passing over a bar, reorganize itself into a new wave with systematic orbital motion. This reorganization is probably the result of dumping the mass of water from the wave crest into the relatively quiet water inside the breaker zone; the impulse generates a new wave. The new wave is smaller than the original one, the difference in heights representing the energy lost in breaking. The new wave, being smaller, proceeds into water equal to 1.3 times its height; then it, too, breaks.

Again a mass of water, white with bubbles of entrained air, is produced, but the water is likely to be too shallow for a new oscillatory wave to form. Now the front of the water becomes a step-shaped wave of translation—a different sort of wave in which the water actually moves forward with the wave form rather than merely oscillating as the wave form passes. Finally, at the beach face, the momentum of the water carries it into an uprush; the water slides and sprawls in a thin swash up and across the face of the beach. As it reaches its uppermost limit the wave dies; all the energy so carefully gleaned from the winds of the distant storm and hoarded for a thousand miles of ocean crossing is gone, expended in a few wild moments. Because the energy is released so rapidly, the energy density in the surf is actually much higher than in the storm which originally created the waves.

The surf changes from moment to moment, day to day, and beach to beach. The waves are influenced by the bottom and the bottom is changed by the waves. And since the waves arriving at a beach are highly variable in height, period, and direction, each wave creates a slightly different bottom configuration for the ones that come after it. The water level changes with the tide and the waves change as the storms at sea develop, shift position, and die out again. The result is that the sand bottom is forever being rearranged. Even in glass-sided wave channels where an endless number of waves, each exactly the same, can be produced, equilibrium is never reached; the sand continues to change as long as the wave machine is running.

Thus the waves change the sand at the same time the sand is changing the waves. First, consider the effect of the bottom on the waves as they break. It may make them plunge or spill.

Plunging breakers are the most impressive. Their principal characteristic is very rapid release of energy from a wave moving at high velocity. There is a sudden deficiency in water ahead of the wave which causes high-velocity currents in the trough as the water rushes seaward to fill the cavity beneath the oncoming crest. When there is not enough water to complete the wave form, the water in the crest, attempting to complete its orbit, is hurled ahead of its steep forward side and lands in the trough. This curling mass of falling water will often entrap air and then, as the upper part of the wave collapses, the air is compressed. When the compressed air finally bursts through the watery cap, a geyser of water is hurled into the air—sometimes over fifty feet. Plate XV shows plunging breakers, and the geysers that sometimes result, better than can be described in words. The entire process lasts only a few seconds.

If there is a strong offshore breeze, the thin crest of the wave will be blown off as it plunges forward, leaving a veil of rising spray behind to mark the path it has followed. This delicate tracery of spray has been likened by poets to the "white manes of plunging horses." Anyone who has observed such breakers, backlighted by a low sun, will understand the comparison and agree that this circumstance is worthy of poetic description.

To understand the reasons why breakers plunge calls for a somewhat more scientific approach. The wave must retain most of its energy right up to the moment of breaking. That is, there should be nothing, such as a rough bottom, a strong wind, or substantial currents, to make the wave prematurely unstable. Any of these conditions will degrade a wave's energy by slowing it down and warping its orbits so that it breaks gradually rather than abruptly. Thus, when a large clearly-defined swell passes over a steep smooth underwater slope of the proper depth on a calm day, a perfect plunging breaker will result. If, however, the bottom is gently sloping and studded with rocky irregularities, or if the approaching waves appear confused, a spilling breaker is more likely to be produced.

A spilling wave breaks slowly and without the violent release of energy needed to fling the crest forward into the trough ahead. Its crest merely tumbles down a more gently-sloping forward side, sometimes over a considerable distance and lasting for several minutes. Therefore, spilling waves are much favored by surfers, who ride on the face of the wave, their boards doing much the same thing the tumbling white water is doing.

The famous surfboarding area at Waikiki, where surfers in outrigger canoes and on boards are frequently photographed against Diamond Head, is a fine place to observe perfect spilling breakers. There a very shallow gently-sloping coral reef extends for a mile outward from the beach. The tide range is very small so that almost all swell coming in from the Pacific is converted into low spilling breakers. The surfer can paddle out as far as he likes and be assured of a ride back at any time.

Most surf zones have larger tidal ranges and are underlain by shifting sand; instead of remaining the same as Waikiki does, their underwater topography is constantly changing. The result is that in most surf zones one can observe some combination of plunging and spilling breakers, and forms which are intermediate between the two. That is, the breaker plunges, but without sufficient momentum to hurl the water beyond the sloping forward side into the trough ahead. The falling curtain of water lands partway down the wave front and the breaker has an "intermediate section."

Some beaches have such a steeply-sloping approach that a swell approaches the shore without being slowed or changed until the last possible moment. Then it will abruptly rise up and break directly on the beach face with astonishing violence. Usually these are plunging breakers.

In other areas the beach approach may shoal so gradually that the surf zone may be as much as a mile wide. On the beaches of Oregon and Washington that have underwater slopes of about 1:100 (one foot vertical to one hundred feet horizontal) it is not unusual to have three lines of breakers when the great winter storm waves arrive. The outer line of breakers may be plunging, thirty feet high, with sufficient violence to shake earthquake-measuring instruments several miles inland. Having broken, they will re-form and break twice more with decreasing violence as they cross a half mile of irregular shallows to reach the shore.

The movement of broken waves in shallow water creates another type of wave, the wave of translation. This wave was first discovered and studied by J. Scott Russell in the 1840s, when it was of much greater scientific interest than at present. The name "solitary wave" is now used by the mathematicians to describe this phenomenon.

Two striking characteristics clearly differentiate the wave of translation from the ordinary oscillatory waves which we have been considering. First, the entire form of this wave is above the undisturbed water level; that is, it consists of a crest without an accompanying trough. Second, there is an actual translation of the water particles as the wave form passes. An object floating in the water would be carried a definite distance forward by a wave of translation and come to rest, without exhibiting the corresponding backward motion observed in the wave of oscillation.

Russell found that the wave of translation is produced by the sudden addition of a mass of water to a still-water surface. When the oscillatory wave breaks, the water in the broken crest falls onto the water surface in advance of the oncoming wave, producing a wave of translation or a step-shaped foamline which continues shoreward. Hence, although this type of wave is nonexistent in the open sea, it becomes important in the shallow waters inside the breakers, where most oscillatory waves eventually are transformed into waves of translation.

These waves travel at the velocity $\sqrt{gd}$ with the unusual variation that, since the wave height is large compared to the depth of water, the two are added to give d. The velocity therefore is related to the water depth, and when there are several waves of translation moving shoreward at the same time, the later ones move faster and tend to overtake the ones ahead because they are traveling in deeper water on top of their predecessors.

SURF BEAT

One of the wave characteristics most evident to an observer standing on the shore is the variability in height of the breakers. A series of a dozen or so low waves will approach and break. Then there will be a group of several high waves—usually three or four —then another relatively quiescent period.

Sometimes this variability is caused by the arrival of two sets of swell (from two storms) of nearly the same period at the same time. When the crests of the two wave trains almost coincide, they reinforce each other and produce waves higher than those of either set. When the waves are almost com-

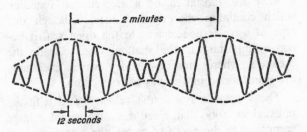

Fɪɢ. 54. Surf beat envelope. Two groups of waves, each about twelve-second period, combine to reinforce and cancel each other, causing a "beat" with a period of two minutes.

pletely out of phase and the crests in one train coincide with troughs in the others, the resulting waves are small. As the phase relationship changes, a pattern emerges like that shown in Figure 54. The envelope of these wave traces (shown dotted) has a wave form and a period or "beat frequency"—usually two to three minutes—but it is not a true long-period wave.

The effect of groups of breakers of alternating height is to raise and lower the average water level in the surf zone. The rise is somewhat exaggerated because the volume of water transported into the surf zone is proportional to the square of the breaker height.

Anyone wading in shallow water notices that a rapid succession of high breakers temporarily raises the water level. John Isaacs says that he has seen variations of sea level of as much as sixteen feet at Twin Rocks, Oregon, in very heavy weather caused by surf beat. The waves of translation resulting from the large breakers transport a considerable volume of water shoreward on the surface faster than it can escape seaward again along the bottom.

The consequence of this process, according to Walter Munk, whose name is conspicuously identified with surf beat, is that the shoreline tends to act as a source of new waves which return about one percent of the incoming wave energy seaward as true long-period waves. These newly-formed waves resulting from surf beat move seaward and along the coast and may be the cause of surging in harbors.

UNDERTOW AND RIP CURRENTS

One of the most ubiquitous myths of the seashore is that of undertow. The very word frightens many would-be surf swimmers, and some beaches have signs which say, "Dangerous Undertow, Swim at

Your Own Risk." Even at beaches without signs, rumors of undertow often have been passed down for several generations without anyone's having experimented to determine the facts.

The author cannot define undertow, but timid souls and uninformed lifeguards assert it is a mysterious current that flows seaward from the beach along the bottom and "sucks (or tows) swimmers under."

There are currents flowing in the surf zone and there are other water motions which may cause trouble for swimmers, but they hardly fit the description given. Consider them one at a time. Orbital currents in the waves perform circles equal to the height of the waves with the period of the waves. A swimmer in waves performs these circles as the water does; half the time these move him down to seaward, the other half up to landward. After each wave passes he is about where he started. If he gets in the trough of a breaker he will indeed be sucked under it, and as it breaks he will be upended and propelled landward, possibly to be cast up on the sand.

The foamlines of broken water (waves of translation) do transport water landward that must somehow return seaward as a current. If the beach has a reasonably even slope inside the bar, there may be a return current on the bottom. But in order for the wave of translation to endure, the water must be quite shallow—perhaps two or three feet. So in most circumstances a swimmer could stand on the bottom and, even if knocked down by the water moving landward, he certainly would not be carried out to sea along the bottom by the relatively small return current.

On very steep beaches where large waves break directly on the beach, the uprush and backrush may be violent surges of water as much as two feet deep. These are quite capable of knocking a man down and rolling him back down the beach into the path of the next breaker, where he could be mauled and tossed about by several waves before he could regain his footing. In such circumstances usually the best escape is to swim seaward and reach the calm water outside the breakers—it is only a few feet away. Once there he can select the right wave and ride it in, sliding far up the beach on the uprush, digging into the sand at the high point and holding there until the backrush draws the water away, then scrambling to high ground before the next uprush. This maneuver can be real sport, though it is a bit dangerous. However, steep beaches with high surf are rare; certainly there are none in the usual resort areas. But this minor hazard does not fit the popular description of undertow.

One time on the beach at Carmel, California, a popular swimming resort, I was discussing the question of undertow with a group of bathers who insisted that it was "very strong" at a certain point they indicated. The sand at Carmel is very white, the water clear; the breakers on this occasion were about seven feet high and a hundred feet offshore. We conducted the following experiment. A packet of life-jacket marker-dye was tied to a cobblestone and heaved into the water some fifty feet from shore in the supposed zone of undertow. After the stone reached bottom, we pulled the dye-release tab, which had been tied to a long string. It was plain to the watchers on the beach face that as the bright green dye spread, the water it marked swayed with each passing wave but showed not the slightest tendency to flow as a current in any direction. This demonstration settled the point at the time, but the undertow warning signs probably are still there, as well as on many other public beaches where they have no more meaning. Such signs are well-intentioned and may warn the swimmer of real danger, but they do not tell him what to do. For this I have a suggestion at the end of this section.

There is one form of current in the surf zone that can be dangerous to an inexperienced swimmer. This is the rip current, first described by F. P. Shepard, of Scripps Institution of Oceanography. The rip is also of importance in beach processes, for it is responsible for some of the strange forms that the underwater parts of a beach may take.

Rip currents are formed when waves break on a shallow underwater bar in rapid succession. The water they hurl shoreward in foamlines cannot easily return seaward along the bottom but "piles up" inside the bar. This excess water is supported there slightly above sea level by the continuous addition of water from more breakers. When the height of water is sufficient, a current starts to flow seaward across the lowest part of the bar. As it moves, it erodes a channel and from then on there is a continuous flow of water called a rip current. The channel may be narrow and the water velocity as high as four feet a second. Rips are supplied with water by feeder currents inside the bar, which collect the water from the foamlines and flow laterally along the beach, as shown in Figure 55. Out beyond the breaker zone, the channel abruptly widens and the strength of the current diminishes. Often it forms a large slow vortex.

Because the depth of water is greater in the rip channel than over the bar on either side, waves rarely

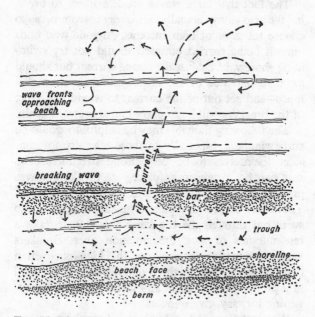

wave fronts approaching beach

breaking wave

rip current

bar

trough

shoreline—

beach face

berm

FIG. 55. Rip currents are created when waves break on a shallow bar making waves of translation which raise the water level inside the bar. The excess water then flows seaward as a swift and narrow rip current in a channel of its own making, ending in a vortex outside the surf.

break in the channel. Moreover, a current flowing against the waves has the effect of increasing wave velocity. The crests become prematurely unstable and a small spilling breaker may result, or, more likely, a large number of short steep waves will develop that look something like wind chop. The result is that rip currents usually can be seen from the beach, especially if one can observe the surf zone from a vantage point.

The fact that large waves are less likely to break in the rip may actually encourage swimmers to choose the zone of high currents. Anyone who finds himself being carried outward should not try swimming shoreward against the strong current but should swim to one side or the other—usually a short distance—and get out of the current to where the effect of the breakers will be to carry him shoreward again.

The following thoughts may be helpful to would-be surf-swimmers, especially to those who do not consider themselves to be very strong swimmers. The surf can be a dangerous place, for breaking waves produce sudden violent forces and swift currents. Therefore, before you plunge in and eagerly try to swim out through the breakers, it is well to take a few minutes to look the situation over. Breakers vary considerably in size, but the high ones often come in groups about three minutes apart. So stand at a proper vantage point and just watch what's happening for, say, five minutes.

Watch the waves break—that's where the bars are. And don't forget that these bars are shallow; you may be able to stand on the bottom in water only waist-deep well out beyond places that are over your head. Generally the lighter-colored foaming water is shallower than the darker water, and it may mark a place where you can rest for a while.

If one is studying waves from the shore, or must decide whether or not to venture out into the surf in a boat, it is useful to be able in advance to judge the

height of the breakers with accuracy. This is easily
done, even if the line of breakers is well offshore.
Simply stand on the beach face at such a level that
the top of the breaker is exactly in line between your
eye and the horizon. Then, as shown in Figure 56,

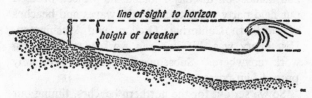

FIG. 56. When the observer's eye is aligned with the top of
the breaker and the horizon, the vertical distance between
the eye and the backrush is equal to the height of the
breaker.

the vertical distance between eye and backrush curl
(which is about at the same level as the average sea
surface) is equal to the height of the breaker. You
may be surprised how high the larger breakers really
are, but it is a lot better to be surprised on the beach
than in their midst.

So, check the height of the breakers, look for rip
currents, and forget undertow.

SURVEYING IN THE SURF

In 1945 I had never seen the ocean, but I joined
the World War II Waves Project of the University of
California at Berkeley. The project had seen set up
to develop scientific means of determining the characteristics of beaches and of the waves that would
make it difficult for landing craft to approach enemy-

held beaches. Studying the surf was our business. Later, when the war was over, the project continued, its objectives becoming more broadly scientific.

M. P. O'Brien, Dean of Engineering and a member of the Beach Erosion Board, directed the work and, almost on the day I joined the project, ordered our field party north to study the waves and beaches of Northern California, Oregon, and Washington. His theory was, "If you can work there, you can work anywhere." Subsequent experience certainly proved him correct.

So we set out for the northern beaches, timing our arrival to coincide with that of the great waves from the winter storms. John Isaacs, an old hand along the coast, was party leader; I was his engineer assistant. Field-party equipment included two amphibious six-wheeled trucks called Dukws (and pronounced ducks), a collection of aerial cameras, walkie-talkie radios, and a Catalina PBY flying boat.

Dukws are fascinating vehicles, thirty-two feet long and eight feet wide, whose top rises ten feet above the roadway. On the highway they are formidable and even the log trucks will give them a fair share of the road, but in the surf they seem no more than a chip of wood. In the water they move by means of a screw propeller, and fortunately they turned out to be probably the world's best surf craft, or else I would not be around to write about them.

John and I each drove a Dukw up the coast—the regular drivers were to join us later—and I well remember on the bleak day we approached Eureka that John stopped his Dukw and motioned for me to join him. He pointed out across Humboldt Bay and the sandspit separating bay from ocean to a sort of white froth on the horizon a couple of miles away where an occasional geyser shot up. "Some of those breakers must be thirty feet high—plunging. Look at them explode!" Then, in a matter-of-fact way, "That's where we're going to work."

Since I had never seen a wave before, much less the Pacific Ocean, I did not quit on the spot but accepted this proposal as a normal part of university research. Thirty-foot breakers sounded like a reasonable size for an ocean as large as the Pacific. Now it seems that even this modest description should at least have generated in my mind a picture of a tumbling wall of water higher than a two-story house breaking into a foaming mass that would compare favorably with the tumult below the spillway at Grand Coulee Dam, but it did not. Having spent my previous working life in mines and tunnels, I was not quite sure what a breaker was.

We set up an observation station at Table Bluff lighthouse, a hundred feet above the beach, and began systematically photographing the waves twice a day and noting their characteristics. Square frames covered with white canvas were anchored into the beach above high tide at thousand-foot intervals. These markers would give scale to the aerial photos and establish the survey lines that we would run out through the surf. On days when the surf was high we would make simultaneous radio-fired photos of the surf zone from the flying boat overhead and from the cliff. Then, when the breakers on the outer bar were low (meaning that most of them were under fifteen feet high), we would survey the bottom along lines extending out from the air markers. The object of all this was, of course, to establish the relationship between the waves and the underwater topography and give us data for future determination, by aerial photography alone, of the nature of the approaches to enemy-held beaches.

The method of surveying the underwater part of the beach was this: We would set up pairs of range boards a hundred feet apart perpendicular to the shoreline so that the Dukw driver could keep the craft on line as it moved slowly landward along the survey line. Down the beach a thousand feet, at a point making a right angle with the range boards, a surveyor's transit was set up to measure readily the angle to the Dukw along the hypotenuse of the triangle. At frequent intervals a leadsman standing in the waist of the Dukw would call, "Mark," into the radio transmitter and heave a lead-weighted sounding line into water off the bow. As the Dukw passed the lead he would hold the line vertically and read off the depth of water beneath the trough of the wave. To this depth he would add the one third of the estimated height of the wave about to break over him and call the total into the microphone.

The transit man, following the progress of the Dukw through the telescope, would, on hearing "Mark" via the radio and seeing the lead splash, read the angle. An assistant at his side would record angle and depth. This established depths at a series of points along a line, so that we could plot a profile of the sand surface beneath the waves. Figure 62 in Chapter IX shows one of hundreds of profiles that were made in this fashion. Since the beach constantly readjusted itself, there was no end to the work.

These jobs were divided in such a manner that Isaacs always ran the transit and Bascom was the

leadsman on these sorties through the surf. Somehow, in innocence and ignorance, I was persuaded
that fifteen-foot breakers smashing down on a thirty-
two-foot tin boat were nothing to be disturbed about.
In reality, of course, we often underestimated the

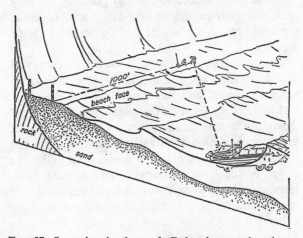

FIG. 57. Surveying in the surf. Dukw is overtaken by a
breaker as it moves landward along a course marked by
range poles. Man in Dukw heaves lead and calls "mark" into
radio followed by measured depth. Transit man on beach
reads angle; an assistant seated by the radio receiver records
both depth and distance.

height and unexpectedly encountered breakers over
twenty feet high. At these times our friends on the
beach offered many helpful suggestions by radio.

Perhaps when the Coast Guardsmen from Humboldt Bay lifeboat station served notice that we were
working at our own risk and could not count on their
help if we got into trouble, I should have been more
wary. They obviously were astonished that anyone

would start out into what they considered to be a raging surf for any reason short of emergency life-saving. But they had the advantage of appreciating the risk, and several years had passed before it dawned on me that we were doing anything daring. We were the first, and to this day probably the only ones, foolhardy enough to take this much interest in the sand beneath the winter surf on northern Pacific beaches.

There was many a close call when a Dukw would almost get sideways to a breaker or have the canvas cover ripped off and the supporting ribs caved in. Dukws have no flotation compartments. If one went down, there was precious little chance—the outer breakers being more than half a mile from shore and the water temperature in the forties—that either the driver or the leadsman would make it back alive. Even though we always wore life jackets, our heavy clothes and the wild turbulence would quickly have exhausted us. On one occasion a breaker heaved the Dukw onto the beach face on its side, wheels pointing out to sea, throwing me clear. The next wave set it back on its wheels without damage. Somehow, no one was ever hurt. We were young and lucky, and in return for the risks we had the fun of challenging the breakers.

In order to "run a line of soundings" it usually was necessary to get out through two major lines of breakers; often we would smash head-on into half a dozen big breakers and be carried backward before a series of smaller waves would arrive and let us cross the bar. At each breaker the Dukw collided with the mass of solid green water moving (relatively) at twenty miles an hour; at the moment of impact each tiny leak in the driver's cockpit was like a firehose turned on the men inside. Often the glass in the windshield would crack or the canvas rip; we nearly always lost the windshield wipers and ended up with the pumps furiously throwing out a stream of water the size of a man's leg. Though each wave washed over us, the Dukw would shudder and rise above the surface; with persistence we would get through. At such times a good strong rip current was appreciated. When these currents existed, they carved channels through the bars, and the water would be too deep for all but the largest swell to break. If the Dukw could get in a rip it had a much better chance of crossing the bar without serious pounding; besides, its speed was increased by that of the current. Amid waves breaking on all sides these passages were hard to identify. We would station a lookout on the bluff who could see the whole surf zone and, by means of the walkie-talkie radios, guide the Dukw into the rip channels, much as aircraft pilots are "talked" through low clouds in ground-controlled-approach. Or sometimes, on approaching the outer line of breakers, we would rest in the quiet zone between the bars and watch the big ones go over for a while—occasionally deciding that the sand could just as well be surveyed on another day. The drivers knew that any serious mistake would be their last one, and it was not unusual for them to quit "for good" when the wheels touched safely down on shore. Then we would talk it over and decide not to sally forth into such large breakers again. Next morning the drivers would be on the job early, ready to go.

Surfboarding on a Dukw is great sport. I well

remember bucking out through the surf just south of the Columbia River entrance, finally getting beyond the outermost breakers and then sitting there for nearly an hour getting up nerve enough to run the breakers. As a trough passed, we could look down a dark watery valley that disappeared into the fog in each direction; then we would be lifted up on the next crest. From this temporary vantage point we could see a dozen more huge crests approaching, and looking landward see the back side of lines of frightening breakers. They were all about the same—nearly twenty feet high. Finally we would pick what we thought were slightly lower waves and make a run for it. Usually our judgment of height was wishful thinking, but for excitement it beats a roller coaster any day: full speed ahead at six knots until you are overtaken by a wall of water as high as a house and moving three times your speed. The trick is to time the run so that the biggest wave breaks just barely ahead of you; then you can ride in atop the breaking crest, crossing the bar just in time to get beyond reach of the next wave. (It's a good idea, but it's hard to put into practice.)

As the wave overtakes the craft, there is a sickening moment when the stern begins to lift rapidly and the driver fights to remain square with the waves (encountering a wave sideways would mean disaster). Then as speed picks up, the craft tilts forward at thirty degrees or so and buries its bow until there is green water across the windshield. The entire craft seems about to flip end-over-end and you think, "Why did I ever get myself in a place like this? What a fool to go to sea in a truck!"

But then the wave begins to pass under, and the

buoyancy of the forward end lifts the bow until it is a level platform projecting out ten to fifteen feet above the slick green water surface of the trough below. The forward wheels and axle hang down so that the rushing water of the breaker crests beats against them from behind and carries this awkward looking truck-boat forward like a surfboard. Now you are flying, perched on a wave making fifteen knots, water boiling on all sides—an exhilarating ride. Taking soundings has become second nature; you heave the lead, estimate the still-water level, call the depth.

Soon the wave sets the craft into the quiet water and continues on, leaving the Dukw to continue at its own speed, still surveying. There is another line of breakers ahead, but these are only ten feet high and now seem tame. Inside at last, the Dukw rides easily and safely on the leading edge of a foamline sometimes five or six feet high. A foamline is a boiling mass of aerated white water; as the air escapes, the mass loses height and only a foot or two of green water reaches the beach face. Once through the inner breakers, the driver engages the wheels, and as the water shoals, the tires touch gently as weight is transferred gradually from the buoyancy of the hull to the truck's springs. Finally, motor roaring and gears grinding, the craft climbs out of the water and lurches to a stop at the backrush to mark the end of the run; then up the beach face, a truck once more. With tire pressure controlled from the cab, a Dukw can operate in the softest sand. Happy to be safe ashore, the crew open the drain plugs to let out the water. They check by radio with the transit party down on the beach to see if all the data were properly received and recorded. "Okay? Now we'll run the next line a thousand feet down the beach."

Although this method of surveying in the surf may seem crude, we would often repeat lines to check on ourselves; even in the rough surf there was rarely a disagreement of more than a foot. Since an echo sounder will not work amid bubbles and turbulence, the old lead-line method seems to be the only technique of obtaining such data.

After several years of almost daily surf operations Isaacs and I wrote a thick pamphlet which became known as the "Dukw report." It went into considerable detail about our experiences with these wonderful vehicles, including the fact that we lost two in the surf and one that rolled off a mountain cliff in Oregon and plunged two hundred feet into the sea. A result of that report about our operations in heavy surf was that the U. S. Coast Guard—which had previously regarded these tin-hulled trucks with some suspicion—began using them for surfboats at their life-saving stations.

The big breakers are so far from shore that we were never able to get very good pictures of the Dukws in really large surf. However, Plate II of the surf zone at Table Bluff was taken with a long focal-length aerial camera and shows the Dukw a mere speck in a breaker over half a mile from shore. In the summer we worked south, often in the Monterey Bay area. There, while training a new driver for the much rougher northern work, we obtained Plate I of a Dukw surfboarding on a modest twelve-foot breaker.

After five years spent largely in observing and recording waves, studying and surveying beaches, and photographing the entire U.S. Pacific coast from ground and air, I recorded the status of the coast as of 1950 in a three-volume tome, *Shoreline Atlas of the Pacific Coast of the U. S.* Many years hence, when the forces of erosion have had time to accomplish notable changes in the coast, this book should form a valuable basis for comparison.

Chapter IX

BEACHES

Along the boundary between land and sea the solid underlying rock is covered with a layer of rock fragments. These fragments range in size from fine sand to large cobbles, in thickness from a few inches to hundreds of feet, in color from clear white to opaque black. These are beach materials. Every coastal dweller in the world is quite sure he knows what a beach is like. Yet if you were to ask, you would find totally different opinions, and all derived from local experience.

BEACH MATERIALS

The open-sea beaches that border much of the United States from Cape Cod south along Jersey and the Carolinas to Florida, and along the California coast south of Point Conception are for the most part composed of coarse, light-colored sand, produced by the weathering of granitic rocks into their two main constituents, quartz and feldspar. Generally these beaches are steep-faced and coarse-grained. Since they contain our most popular beach resorts, many Americans tend to think that they fairly represent the world's beaches. But hundreds of miles of beach along the Oregon-Washington coast are quite different. There the sand is fine-grained and dark gray-green in color, derived from the weathering of basalt, which forms beaches that are wide, flat, and often hard as a racetrack. Much of the Florida coast is equally hard and fine-grained, but it comes from the disintegration of coral.

On the other hand, the beach at Cannes in southern France is largely composed of uncomfortable pebbles, and much of the English coast is lined with small flat stones called shingle. In fact, the word beach seems to have been the ancient word for a shingle shore.

Many beaches of Labrador and Argentina are composed of large cobbles. Those of Lower California are composed of two materials, a flat sandy portion that is exposed only at low tide, while above and behind the sand great cobble steps called ramparts rise to a height of thirty feet or more. On Tahiti, if you live on the windward side of the island, you think it is natural for a beach to be made of black volcanic sand. But if you live on the other side, where the wide coral reef furnishes the beach material, it seems reasonable for beaches to be blindingly white. In fact, beaches can be made of nearly any material that is present in quantity; rock fragments are not necessarily required. At Fort Bragg, California, a small pocket-beach consists entirely of old tin cans washed in from the city's nearby oceanic dump and arranged by the waves into the usual beach forms, as though to prove that the laws of beach physics cover all possibilities.

Thus, although beaches vary widely in appearance

and composition, the principles that govern their behavior are the same, and for convenience here all beach materials will be called sand. The accompanying table shows the actual sizes of the particles and may help the reader to visualize the beaches being discussed relative to those within his own experience. Several other factors, including the shape and density of the particles, are of interest but they are of secondary importance.

A beach responds with great sensitivity to the forces that act upon it—waves, currents, winds. It is a deposit of material in transit, either alongshore or off- and onshore. The important thought in the definition is that of motion, for beaches are ever-changing, restless armies of sand particles, always on the move. Most sand movement occurs under water, the result of waves and wave-caused currents that organize the particles into familiar forms. But the motion of a beach before the waves, even when huge quantities of sand shift in a single day, may not be noticed by a casual observer. The short-term changes are usually imperceptible.

Watch the waves break on a sandy beach; the water runs up the beach face a short way; some of it sinks in, the rest slides back down as the backwash. The moving water carries a film of sand in each direction, and the question is, what is the net effect? Is sand being added to or subtracted from the beach face?

For any small number of waves no one can give a positive answer; each wave is slightly different in height or velocity and may either add or take away a few grains of sand. But overnight, or after a week, the net effect of the waves may be easily observable.

Now you notice that a rock is covered (or uncovered) by sand; you see a small vertical cliff cut into the berm or a newly-added ridge of sand along the beach face; a little way offshore the waves break in a different place, indicating that the bar has shifted. The sand feels different beneath your feet—a new layer of sand, not yet compacted by the waves, is soft to walk on. These are evidence of beach motion; whenever there are waves there is constant shifting, constant readjustment.

This chapter deals only with the offshore-onshore motion of sand. Littoral transport, or the flow of a stream of tumbling particles of sand alongshore under the influence of wave-caused currents, is described in Chapter X.

TABLE VIII

SIZES OF BEACH MATERIALS

(U. S. Corps of Engineers standard)

	Millimeters			
Boulders	Larger than 200			(over 8 inches)
Cobbles	76	to	200	(3 to 8 inches)
Gravel				
Coarse	79	to	76	(includes shingle
Fine	5	to	19	and pebbles)
Sand				
Coarse	2	to	5	
Medium	0.4	to	2	
Fine	0.07	to	0.4	
Silt or clay	Less than .074			(barely visible to naked eye)

SAND MOTION

The principal beach forms are shown in Figure 58, which is a generalized profile of the conditions that prevail in winter and in summer on many beaches exposed to the ocean. Remember that our definition of beaches includes all the sand in motion above and below water out to a depth of about thirty feet. Above water there is usually a nearly horizontal terrace of sand brought ashore by the waves: the berm. Below water are elongated mounds of sand that parallel the beach: called bars, or sometimes longshore bars.

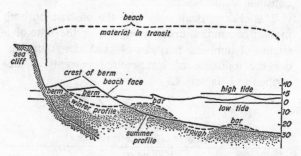

FIG. 58. Generalized profile through an intermediate slope beach showing seasonal changes in the distribution of the sand.

In summer the berm is low and wide. To the layman it *is* the beach—the observable sand on which beach-goers sunbathe and frolic. At that time the underwater profile is likely to be smooth and barless.

In winter the berm is higher and narrower, as most of the sand moves underwater to create the bars. The reason for the shift is the change in wave action with the season. The large waves that come from winter storms cut the berm back; the small waves of summer replace it again. If the amount of sand involved is constant, as it is on a beach between two rocky head-

PLATE XIII. Steep-faced berm at the Carmel River mouth gives way to the relatively flat beach face on which the author is standing. The height of the berm is evidence of the height of the waves that created it. (Bascom)

PLATE XIV. Steep cobbles at Tillamook Head, Oregon,
grade into hard flat sand. (Bascom)

PLATE XV. Waves about ten feet high break directly on the beach face at Carmel River with explosive force, throwing water fifty feet into the air. (University of California)

PLATE XVI. Cusps on the flat fine-grained beach at San Simeon, California. (University of California)

PLATE XVII. Cusps on the steep coarse-grained beach near Monterey, California. (University of California)

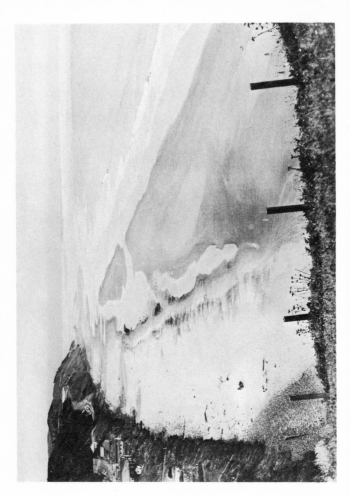

PLATE XVIII. An extreme low tide has exposed this classic example of a longshore bar and rip channel on the beach at Cape Meares, Oregon. The berm, wide and light-colored, slopes abruptly into the flooded trough. (University of California)

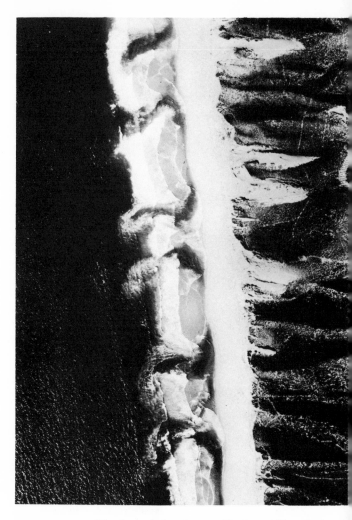

PLATE XIX. Rip channels in a terrace-like bar at Fort Ord, California. Note the absence of breakers in the deep channels. (University of California)

PLATE XX. Sand domes and pinholes. (Bascom)

PLATE XXI. Backwash marks. (Bascom)

PLATE XXII. Swash marks. (Bascom)

PLATE XXIII. Bars and ripple marks created in an experimental wave channel at the Beach Erosion Board laboratory. (Corps of Engineers)

PLATE XXIV. Large waves spill over the bow of a Coast Guard patrol ship. (U. S. Coast Guard)

lands, the entire beach motion is merely an exchange of sand between berm and bar.

Therefore the study of beaches that are closed systems is concerned principally with the questions of why the sand moves in each direction, which waves are responsible, and what shapes and slopes the sand takes. There is a rather delicate balance between the forces that tend to bring sand ashore and those that move it seaward. The position of the main mass of sand is a measure of the dominant forces.

The basic mechanism is simply the lifting of the individual sand grains from the bottom by the turbulence accompanying the passage of a wave. A sand grain weighs little, since it is lighter under water than in air (by an amount equal to the weight of the water it displaces) and not much energy is required to lift it. Moreover, because of the turbulence and viscosity of the water, the grains settle slowly. While grains are in suspension, or falling freely, currents of very low velocity can move them sidewise. Each time a sand grain is lifted it lands in a slightly different location. Uncounted millions of sand grains are picked up and relocated by every wave, and the beach constantly shifts position. They need not move very far each time, for there are some eight thousand waves a day. Sand grains that move a tenth of an inch per wave could migrate seventy feet in a day. Of course, all waves do not have the same effect, and the currents may change direction. Hence, it is difficult to say whether the sand is moving to or from shore at any moment.

The key to the relation between waves and sand motion is the large change in the beach between winter and summer. Clearly there is a difference in the kind of waves, but what is it? In winter the waves are large and the surf is rough; suspended sand can be seen boiling up behind a breaking wave. Energy is being expended on the beach at a higher rate than in summer. This rate of delivery of energy is most conveniently described in terms of wave steepness—the ratio of wave height to wave length, commonly written H/L.

For example, a six-foot wave six hundred feet long has a steepness of 6/600 or 0.01. If the wave length is only two hundred feet, six-foot waves have a steepness of 0.03. Thus wave steepness increases either with an increase in height or a decrease in length. In wave-channel experiments J. W. Johnson of the University of California at Berkeley was able to show that when the wave steepness is greater than 0.03, bars always formed (starting with a barless beach profile). If the steepness was less than 0.025, bars never formed in the model tank. Probably on a real beach the values are different, but the essential idea is the same. There the waves are highly variable in both height and period, in contrast to those in the model tank which are all precisely the same. Moreover, it is difficult to assess the effect of sand size, which, if scaled down to conform to the rest of the model, would be too small to react properly.

The effect of wave steepness seems to be as follows. When the waves approaching the beach are small (or the wave length is long) the sand on the bottom moves shoreward with the orbital currents. These low-steepness waves pick the sand up, move it forward, and set it down. Although the orbiting water returns seaward an equal distance, the sand it carries is now more likely to be dragged along the bottom. Friction against other sand grains and the existence of a laminar, or non-turbulent, flow region at the bottom keep the sand from moving quite as far as the water does and thus from completing the orbit. Consequently the net motion of sand is landward when the steepness is small.

When relatively large waves follow close upon one another, an entirely different set of circumstances exists. Now there is general turbulence in the surf zone, which keeps the sand in suspension, particularly in shallower water. The mass transport of water by the high waves is greater, and when they break, substantial waves of translation are generated. The result of these effects is that there is a general flow of water shoreward along the surface. Since the waves are relatively close together, the berm remains saturated, and relatively little of the water traveling up and down the beach face sinks into the sand. The shoreward-moving water carries a load of suspended sand particles, and when the waves rush up the beach face, their leading edges surmount the crest of the berm and deposit their sand atop the berm, raising its height. The remainder of the water rushes back down the beach face, picking up a thin layer of sand as it goes. This sandy suspension becomes involved at the bottom with the seaward-flowing currents, which must, of course, balance the landward-moving water at the surface. These currents move the sand seaward until they reach the breaker zone, where the landward-flowing currents are generated. There they deposit their load to form a bar. (Note that this current, while strong enough to influence suspended sand, could not be detected by a swimmer.)

Thus we have an explanation of how the steep winter surf can build the berm higher while cutting it back, and how bars are formed by the erosion of the berm.

The difficulty in determining whether a berm is retreating or advancing at any moment comes from

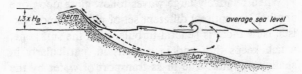

FIG. 59. Circulation of water in surf as steep waves transform dashed profile to solid profile by moving sand from berm to bar.

wave variability—the difference in height and length from wave to wave. Suppose that the waves arriving at a beach all have about the same period and wave length but that the height varies as it does in the examples of Figure 51, Chapter VII. The small waves would bring sand ashore; the large ones would take it away. And that is the way with beaches. The sand is constantly shifting in accordance with complicated and variable water motion. The profile of the sand itself is a rough analogue solution to the question: Is the average wave steepness above or below 0.03?

BERMS AND BARS

Now, equipped with a general understanding of the mechanics of sand migration in the surf zone, we can examine more perceptively the beach forms that are produced. To do this one takes a series of profiles of a beach over a period of time and examines the changes. Over the same period the waves reaching the beach are observed and recorded. The idea is to correlate the beach changes with some specific quality of the waves. It is not easy either to obtain the information or to make sense out of it. But eventually the persistent researcher does end up with an accumulation of data and a "feel" for the way that waves and beaches interact.

The Waves field party eventually surveyed beaches at some forty Pacific Coast locations, repeating pro-

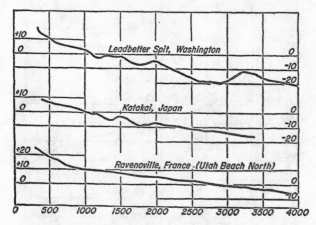

Fig. 60. Profiles of flat beaches. Note the three bars on the beach at Leadbetter Spit. (Slope exaggerated 1:5)

files at some of them dozens of times in many kinds of weather conditions and in all seasons of the year. On each visit we surveyed three lines a thousand feet apart extending from the dunes to minus thirty feet of water to insure obtaining a representative profile. In the course of five years about five hundred profiles were made and six hundred sand samples were taken. Figures 60, 61, and 62 contain a few examples of steep, intermediate, and flat beaches that we profiled and compared with beaches elsewhere in the world. Since beaches are very irregular

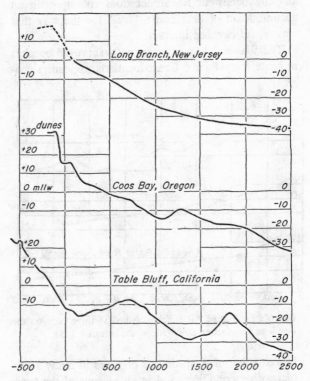

FIG. 61. Intermediate slope beaches. Contrast the barless beach profile at Long Branch with the two huge bars at Table Bluff. (Slope exaggerated 1:5)

194

in slope, the words steep and flat are relative. As used here a flat beach is one on which the water is less than ten feet deep one thousand feet seaward of the zero tide level (mean lower low water), whereas a steep beach is over thirty feet deep one thousand

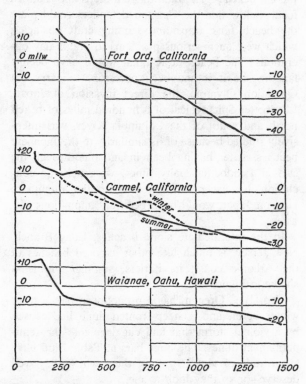

Fig. 62. Profiles of steep beaches. At Waianae only the beach face is sand. The flat area is a coral reef over which great breakers form and where the surfing is excellent (for an expert). (Exaggerated 1:2.5)

feet out from a similar point. Note the difference in vertical exaggeration between the figures.

Each of these beach profiles was selected because it is of special interest. Utah beach, a principal landing point in the invasion of Europe, is among the flat beaches. The tidal range there is about fifteen feet. At low tide the German defenders could plant the beach tank traps and landing craft obstacles, which were such serious problems to our D-day operations. The beach at Katakai would have been a landing site if it had been necessary to carry out Operation Olympic, the direct invasion of Japan. Leadbetter Spit, typical of a hundred miles of beach north and south of the Columbia River, was intensively studied because of its similarity to the Japanese beaches. After having been in and out through the surf at Leadbetter many times, we reach the conclusion that except in very low surf the attempt to land on Japan would have been an amphibious disaster.

In the intermediate slope beaches, Long Branch, New Jersey, is much like other exposed beaches of the Atlantic coast; its barless, summer profile is shown in Figure 61.

Coos Bay, Oregon, has a pronounced bar, a clear winter berm, and a steep-fronted dune line caused by a violent storm that had cut deep into the semi-permanent dunes. The huge bars at Table Bluff have an attitude of violence about them which they well deserve—or so they look to me.

The steep beaches, particularly Fort Ord, demonstrate the extreme. There it is not unusual for waves to break with great violence directly on the beach face, impelling a thick uprush or "surge" of water up and across the beach that can be dangerous to both swimmers and landing craft. A similar situation exists at Waianae, except that the breakers move shoreward across a long flat shoal before they reach the beach face. When the great Pacific swell rolls in, the surfing champions gather to compete.

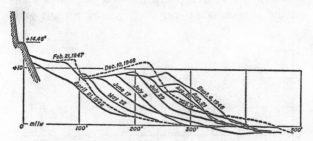

Fig. 63. The berm at Carmel, California, builds two hundred feet seaward during summer when the waves are small. Then it retreats almost to the vanishing point before the large waves of winter storms.

But much of our data came from Carmel, where we would rest in the spring to recover from winter encounters with the northern surf. The beach is a closed system, since it is protected by headlands at each end and by a deep reef offshore. Even there, ten-foot breakers are not unusual. Throughout much of 1946 we maintained a careful watch on that beach in an attempt to keep a "budget" of the sand position—that is, to know where all the sand was all the time. Figure 63 shows the growth of the berm. In the five months between April and September it widened by more than two hundred feet. By December the first large storm had caused the beach face to retreat substantially, but by February it was al-

197

most back to the point of beginning. We were also able to detect berm growth by making precise surveys hour by hour and observed rates of over six feet a day. When storms start to erode the berm, particularly during neap tides, it is not unusual for a steep sandy cliff or scarp to form at the seaward edge of the berm. A vertical scarp five feet high was seen on the Oregon coast—cut overnight by a short and

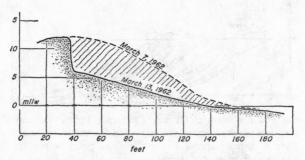

Fig. 64. Typical erosion pattern of Delaware beaches during the great storm of March 6–8, 1962. Many miles of beach retreated sixty to seventy-five feet. (Corps of Engineers profile)

violent storm. On our next survey, two weeks later, small waves had replaced most of the eroded material and only the upper foot of scarp remained. The beach face, of course, is immediately seaward of this scarp, and its slope is actually flattened by the pounding waves.

Since berms are formed by wave action, it is not surprising that the height of the crest of the berm is a function of the height of the waves. Experiments by R. A. Bagnold of England in a wave channel demonstrated that the height of the berm above sea level

198

is 1.3 times the height of the (deep water) waves that formed it. A similar relationship also exists in nature, but it is difficult to confirm because sea level constantly changes with the tides, because refraction influences the amount of deep-water wave energy that reaches any beach, and because every wave is different. However, it seems likely that on ocean beaches the height of the berm is about equal to 1.3 times the significant height of the deep-water waves multiplied by the refraction coefficient. For example, the berm on the continuous beach rimming the gently curved shore of Monterey Bay is sixteen feet above low water at the exposed Fort Ord section and decreases gradually in height toward protected Monterey harbor, where it is six feet lower.

Even a casual beach-watcher soon notices that the slope of the beach face and the size of the sand are

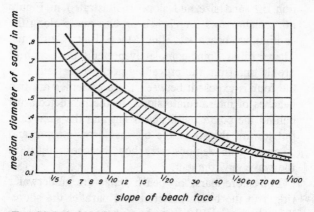

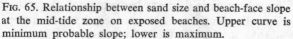

Fig. 65. Relationship between sand size and beach-face slope at the mid-tide zone on exposed beaches. Upper curve is minimum probable slope; lower is maximum.

199

somehow related. Steep beach, coarse sand; flat beach, fine sand. But determining more precisely what the relationship is took quite a while. There are lots of places on a beach to take sand samples and to measure slope, and on the same beach the results vary greatly from place to place. A good deal of sampling and measuring was done before a "reference point" was selected. If the sand sample is taken on the beach face in the zone subjected to wave action at mid-tide and the slope is measured at the same place, consistent results are obtained. Figure 65 shows the relationship for *exposed* beaches. Here again the effects of wave energy cause variations. If the berm is retreating before the pounding of the waves, the slope is less steep than if sand is being added.

A more important effect of exposure to wave action on sand size and slope is illustrated in Figure 66, which shows four beach profiles made along the continuous beach at Half Moon Bay, California. There, Pillar Point completely protects the beach at profile one from the prevailing northwest swell. Profile four is exposed; between these extremes are two beaches of intermediate slope. In the protected zone behind the point, the beach is flat and the sand fine, but toward the south the beaches grow steeper and coarser. This demonstrates how beaches adjust to the wave environment.

Longshore bars, or beach bars, are underwater ridges in the beach material that parallel the shoreline. Often more than one bar is present, the number depending on the size of the waves, the bottom slope, and the tide range. We have discussed already how they are formed by currents that flow when steep

storm waves arrive. Once formed, bars have a pronounced effect on the waves. Because they are abrupt
shoals, they tend to act as filters causing all waves

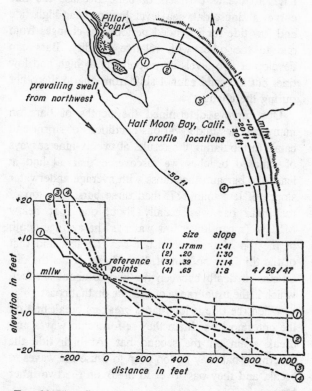

FIG. 66. The effect of a protecting headland on beach slope
and sand size.

above a certain size to break at one spot (instead of
breaking over a wide zone as they would on an even
slope). Moreover, since bars rise abruptly and slope

201

steeply to seaward, they tend to make the breakers plunge and release the energy suddenly.

A substantial range of tide (of five feet or more) tends to create two sets of bars. Because the tide curve is sinusoidal, sea level lingers near high tide and low tide for extended periods but changes from one to the other with relative rapidity. Bars can develop at two levels corresponding to high and low tide, but the sand cannot shift from one to the other during the change.

Our surveys determined the depths of bars on many beaches under various conditions of storm and calm. In tabulating the results of twenty-nine surveys of exposed beaches we discovered that all had at least one bar and that those with average underwater slopes of less than 1:75 had three bars. The top of the inner bar was usually about one foot below MLLW (mean lower low water). The average depth of the top of the second bar was 7.5 feet and that of the third, or outermost, bar 13 feet. Thus the difference in depth between the bars is about six feet, which is the usual range of the tide on that coast.

When the tide is low, large breakers break first on the outermost bar; then they re-form into waves and break again on the second bar. At high tide the outermost bar may be too deep to cause the waves to break, and they pass over to break on the two inner bars.

The deepest bars formed by great storm waves remain unchanged through months of calm weather because small waves do not reach deep enough to rearrange the sand. Even after the most violent storms we never found bars with crests deeper than twenty feet below MLLW, and we concluded that this was their probable maximum depth.

Like other beach features, bars have greater relief when they are made of coarser sand. That is, the troughs between bars are deeper and the slopes steeper. Various attempts to correlate bar spacing with wave length or to find a simple relationship between depth of bars and troughs have not been successful. Since longshore currents often flow in the troughs, these may be scoured deeper or filled in, independent of wave action.

Bars have been observed on beaches ranging in size from model tanks to lakes and oceans, and subject to corresponding wave actions. As many as five have been observed on a single beach, and substantially unbroken bars twenty miles long have been observed on Leadbetter Spit, Washington. But although they have been described here as if they were continuous parallel beach features, often they are very irregular. When wave direction changes, the bars begin to shift position; if the waves quiet down before the shift is complete, the result may be an indescribably ragged arrangement of sand which will remain until the next storm produces order again.

The question of the maximum depth at which the bottom material can be moved by wave action is not settled, in spite of the arbitrary thirty feet below low tide used herein. For example, a violent storm at Madras, India, cast up on shore a quantity of pig lead that came from a vessel wrecked more than a mile offshore. Shingle and chalk ballast dumped overboard by sailing ships in water over sixty feet deep and more than seven miles from shore was brought ashore at Sunderland, England, by wave action. And captains of ships passing over Nantucket shoals, where the depth is seventy-five feet and more, report that storm waves breaking over the ship leave sand on deck. What is the mechanism of transport? No one knows exactly.

MINOR BEACH FEATURES

There are several beach features that seem to have no great geological or engineering importance, but they add interest to the study of beaches. These include swash marks, backwash marks, rills, steps, cusps, domes, pinholes, and ripple marks.

A wonderful time to observe these features is early in the morning, especially after a high tide. Often the air is still and a pleasant light fills the sky. The beach is clean and virginal, the night's waves having erased the human marks of the previous day. Then, with the sand surface free of confusion, beach-watching is most rewarding.

The flow of a thin sheet of water up the beach face that follows the final breaking of each wave on the shore is called the uprush, or sometimes the swash. At its upper edge, just before its energy is spent in the upward motion, the swash is only a film of water less than a quarter of an inch deep. Immediately ahead of the moving water is a line of sand particles, usually a little larger than most of those on the beach face, bulldozed along by the edge of the swash.

When the momentum of the moving water is spent in upward motion, the uprush stops. Part of the water sinks into the sand and part of it slides backward down the beach as the backrush. As it does so, a thin line of sand grains is left to mark its maximum upward reach. These are swash marks.

Swash marks are a sort of scorecard of the reach of a succession of waves. As the general level of surf rises and falls with surf beat, carrying on it

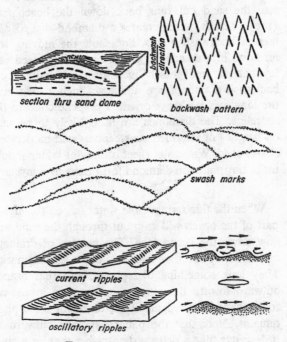

section thru sand dome

backwash direction

backwash pattern

swash marks

current ripples

oscillatory ripples

FIG. 67. Small beach features.

large and small waves, you can watch the marks change position. As the level recedes and successively smaller waves create uprushes, the swash marks make a pattern like that shown in Figure 67.

But as the amplitude of the waves increases, suddenly one larger wave will erase all the previous marks, using their sand grains to make its own record mark. On a receding tide the highest marks remain until the next incoming tide, when a new series, erasing and replacing, climbs up the beach face.

The part of the swashing water that does not sink into the sand but runs back down the beach face (the backrush) often creates a diamond-shaped pattern of backwash marks. Somehow the moving water flows in a manner to create tiny crisscrossed valleys about one fourth inch deep. Usually these backwash diamonds are about six inches long, and the long axis is always oriented perpendicular to the shoreline. The diamonds are most likely to be seen on beaches of intermediate steepness and moderately coarse sand. Why a flat sheet of moving water should make tiny gullies in diamond form remains a mystery.

* * *

When the tide retreats, the water left on the higher part of the beach will seep out through the sand and flow down the beach face. The pattern of drainage of these tiny river systems is known as rill marks. They look something like plant stems that branch outward toward the sea and, when seen in ancient rocks, have been repeatedly mistaken for fossil plant remains. Note that the pattern spreads outward as it descends, like a delta system rather than as a river system in which tributaries join to enlarge the main stream.

When found in sandstones of other geologic periods, swash marks, rill marks, and backwash marks are not only excellent evidence that the sand once was the beach of a prehistoric sea, they also point the direction of the sea and indicate the range of tide.

* * *

As the backrushing water slides down the surface of the beach its velocity increases and the surface sand grains are lifted into suspension. The momentum of this turbid sheet of water and sand carries it below the general level of the sea, and a small wave, usually less than a foot high, called the backrush breaker, curls over it. The result is a turbulent sandy swirl whose effect is to lift the sand grains and keep them in suspension, to be carried up the beach face again by the next uprush. But the larger sand grains may settle to the bottom, where they roll back and forth as each wave passes, occasionally being lifted and dropped again by unusually violent water motion. The net effect of this constant shifting is segregation according to size in which the larger particles move steadily downward. A little below the level of the lowest backrush breaker these larger sand grains reach a depth at which they can no longer be moved upward by most of the waves. The result is a step-like deposit whose upper surface is the continuation of the beach face and whose outer surface is the angle of repose of the sand. This low-tide step, which is usually about a foot high, may be hard to see because of the turbulence, but it is often encountered with momentary alarm by the bare feet of waders who sink into the soft, coarse sand or step off its abrupt edge.

* * *

Cusps are evenly-spaced crescent-shaped depressions concave to seaward that are built by wave action on the seaward edge of the berm. Of all the curiosities of the shore these are surely the most puzzling, and none of the dozens of explanations that have been given for their formation is completely satisfying. Cusps varying greatly in shape have been observed in beaches made of fine sand and large cobbles; they occur equally in protected bays and on exposed beaches. Cusps have been made in the laboratory with lengths of six to nine inches; they have been measured by the author at San Simeon, California (fourteen feet), at Fort Ord (ninety feet), and at Table Bluff (average of nine measured with a Dukw milometer—1180 feet).

Like other beach features, cusps have more striking relief and are less regular on exposed beaches made of coarse sand than in protected bays, where the precision of cusps sculpted in fine sand on a flat beach is a thing to marvel at. They seem to the author to develop at wave steepnesses between erosion and deposition. In fact, their shape suggests indecision or perhaps nearly-balanced forces of alternate dominance.

There is no general agreement on how cusps form or why they should be the shapes and sizes they are, but the rankest amateur can stand for half an hour watching wave action in cusps and convince himself he knows how the cusps are maintained. The two-wave cycle is often something like this (Figure 68). On the even wave a straight swash, (1) bearing its usual load of suspended sand, rushes up the beach face. It is split into segments by the apex points and deflected along the sides of the bay until its force is spent or it meets the water of the opposite side. (2) Once stopped, it is influenced solely by gravity and returns seaward by the steepest path, which (3) leads it to the channel in the center of the bay. The considerable velocity of the water down this channel moves bottom material, (4) and a small submarine delta forms. The effect of this jet of water is to stop abruptly the water it meets in front of the next wave,

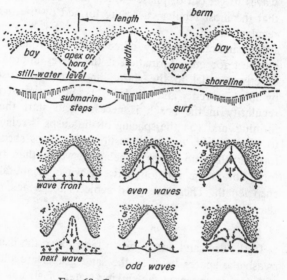

FIG. 68. Cusps are a puzzlement.

(5) making that wave relatively ineffective at shifting sand. Even so, the part of that wave opposite the horn is unimpeded and, as before, it rushes up and drops its sand.

It should be noticed that the high backrush velocity and the low slope associated with the removal of sand from a beach exist only in the channel, whereas the highest uprush velocities and lowest saturation are found at the horn, which is steep and depositional. The cycle repeats. Apparently cusp horns are built by every wave and the bays are deepened by the work of every other wave. Of course, this two-wave cycle does not repeat every time because variability in wave height and period causes the waves to get out of phase—which may be the reason that the most regular cusps are formed by the most regular waves.

Researchers generally agree that (1) conditions are best for cusp formation if the waves approach exactly parallel to the shore, and are unconfused by local currents and winds, (2) some original irregularity in the beach is necessary to start them forming, and (3) the spacing of the cusps is related to wave height. But the question why cusps should form at all is no closer to being answered than before, nor is the relation between wave height and cusp length. These are good subjects for beach researchers.

* * *

In the dry sand on the beach face above the usual swash the spaces between the sand grains are filled with air. In this area the sinking water of an unusually long uprush will cause sand domes and pinholes to form. This happens when the thin layer of uprush water sinks vertically and displaces the air. The air then migrates upward and emerges from pinholes in the sand surface as a chain of bubbles. The water swashing across the pinholed surface in subsequent uprushes sinks down through the holes and smooths them into tiny temporary funnels about an eighth of an inch in diameter.

The first of the high uprushes, however, may be

sufficient only to wet the sand to a depth of about half an inch, making a relatively impervious layer with air trapped beneath. When the next uprush comes and its water sinks downward, the air beneath the saturated zone is forced together in pockets as before. But now the sand surface is sealed, and instead of the air escaping as a series of small bubbles, it becomes one large bubble. Unable to escape as the pressure rises, the bubble lifts the sand above it into a low dome perhaps a quarter of an inch in height and three inches across or sometimes twice that large. One can tap these domes with a finger and feel them collapse, or slice them carefully with a pocket knife and see the dome structure.

* * *

Sand subjected to the action of moving water frequently forms parallel ridges and troughs which are known as ripple marks. They are like small waves of sand and may be seen in sandy stream bottoms, on the face of a gently-sloping beach when the tide is out, and beneath the surf zone. Ripple marks are commonly seen in ancient strata (sometimes with dinosaur tracks), and they have been photographed on the ocean floor in water eighteen thousand feet deep. In short, whenever there is sand under water, ripples may be formed by the motion of the water. They come in a great variety of shapes and sizes.

Ripple "wave length" may be as little as two inches and the height a fraction of an inch, or they may form sand waves several feet deep and fifty or more feet long. Ordinarily ripples are only a few inches from crest to crest and their size seems to be related to the size of the sand from which they are formed, the velocity of the current, and the amount of material in suspension.

Observation and carefully controlled experiments reveal that there are two well-defined kinds of ripples: (1) Current ripples, which are formed by water flowing in a single direction, are asymmetrical with a long gentle slope on the side from which the current comes and short steep slope on the lee side. (2) Oscillation ripples, created by the equal back-and-forth currents of flattened orbits at the bottom as oscillatory waves pass above, are symmetrical. The ripple marks seen on beaches are almost always a complicated mixture of the two, since orbit size varies from wave to wave and the direction of bottom currents usually is highly variable.

Since wave fronts generally parallel the shoreline, it might be expected that the underwater ripples would also parallel the shore, but this is true only part of the time. Even beneath the surf the asymmetrical current ripples seem to predominate. There, if the ripples are observed relative to a peg driven into the bottom, they are seen to be constantly in motion in an explicably random manner and direction. Probably they are a prime mechanism in the movement of sand by water, but unfortunately ripples do not clearly indicate the direction of the main migration.

In fact, although the sand moves in the direction of the current, the ripple form does not. If the velocity of the moving water is more than about 2.2 feet a second, the vortex motion in the lee of the crest causes the ripple form to move against the current. When the velocity exceeds 2.5 feet per second the ripples are swept away entirely as in an underwater sandstorm.

Chapter X

THE LITTORAL CONVEYOR BELT

The movement of sand along a coast by wave-caused currents, called littoral transport, is responsible for most shoreline problems. Either sand is being removed from some place that people wish it would stay or it is being deposited some place where it is not wanted, or both. The processes are as old as the ocean and, by man's usual standards, fairly slow; that is, years are usually required to make an appreciable change. As long as the property bordering the ocean is in the form of great ranches or public lands, no one pays much attention to a change in the position of the shoreline of fifty feet over a period of fifty years. Its exact position is usually not known and no great value is assigned to the land. When, however, a lighthouse or road is built near the water's edge so that there is a fixed object against which shoreline changes can be conveniently measured, the coastal dwellers first become dismayed by the loss of land, then alarmed.

When the ranches are subdivided into small lots on the edge of the sea cliff and sold for high prices, as has happened at many places on the California coast, the new owners are soon in an uproar when they find their land is disappearing at the rate of a foot

213

a year. The process of erosion has not changed, only the attitude toward it. Something must be done at once!

In England in the early 1900s property owners whose land was being eroded by wave action clamored for the Government to take preventive action. Their island was disappearing beneath the sea! They argued so loudly that a Royal Commission was appointed to study the matter. After making a careful survey, the commission reported that over a period of thirty-five years England and Wales lost 4692 acres and gained 35,444 acres, giving a net gain of nearly nine hundred acres a year. This finding seemed to prove that people whose land disappeared complained more loudly than those whose land was increasing. It must be admitted, however, that the land lost probably was good cliffland on the open coast which disappeared in a spectacular way, whereas the land gained was low, sandy and not particularly valuable. Non-geologists are usually not aware that the very existence of a cliff is warning that erosional processes are at work, even though the changes seem to be very slow.

It is said that George Washington studied the erosion of the Long Island coast and ordered that the Montauk Point lighthouse at the eastern tip be built at least two hundred feet back from the edge of the cliff so it would last two hundred years. At the present rate of erosion it will just about last that long. A recent measurement showed about forty feet left between the base of the lighthouse and the edge of the cliff.

Unfortunately, almost anything that either speeds up erosion of a coast or retards the normal motion of sand alongshore affects all the other property within the same littoral zone. Any "remedial" action that does not consider the effects on the downstream beaches only causes more problems. Thus the shoreline engineer, in addition to considering the complex immediate problem of what action to take at any one place to keep the property owners there happy, must be careful that his solution does not create worse problems somewhere else. The best he can hope for is a good solution for a few generations; eventually the long-term geological process will overwhelm anything he does.

SHORELINE EROSION

There are several mechanisms by which the sea attacks a cliff and makes sand. These are: (1) hydraulic and pneumatic action in which the pressure of water moving at high velocity against the cliff forces water into cracks in the rock and compresses the air that is trapped (this compressed air will sometimes shove large blocks of rock *away* from the cliff into the waves); (2) the impact of water laden with rock fragments, which act as cutting tools against the cliff; (3) the abrasion or rubbing together of the fragments in suspension; (4) grinding of the blocks that fall against each other as the cliff is undercut; and (5) corrosion or chemical weathering of salt water and oxygen in the zone just above sea level.

Exactly how does rock become sand?

A vivid picture of the working of the "sea mill," which grinds large boulders to fine sand, was given by J. W. Henwood in an account of the visit he made to a mine that extended out under the sea in south-west England: "When standing beneath the base of the cliff, and in that part of the mine where but nine feet of rock stood between us and the ocean, the heavy roll of the larger boulders, the ceaseless grinding of the pebbles, the fierce thundering of the billows, with the crackling and coiling as they rebounded, placed a tempest in its most appalling form too vividly before me to be ever forgotten. More than once doubting the protection of our rocky shield we retreated in affright; and it was only after repeated trials that we had confidence to pursue our investigations."

Few persons are privileged to listen to the surf from below, but similar sounds are created by large waves breaking in pocket beaches on steep rocky coasts. Where cliffs rise vertically from the sea there are often slot-like depressions carved by the waves and floored with cobble beaches. Watching from the cliff above, one sees a wave break violently in the slot with much hissing and roaring. The churning water lifts cobbles as though they were sand grains and carries them upward in a surge of green and white froth. When this happens one hears muffled "clocks" as the cobbles strike against each other. Then, at the top of the uprush, water and cobbles crash against the base of the cliff and the wave reflects. Down goes the water again, dragging its load of cobbles, causing them to clatter against one another with a loud crackling sound. The observer is readily impressed by the violence trapped in the pocket and finds no difficulty thereafter in understanding how beaches have been created from cliffs by the relentless impacting and grinding of waves.

As the rocks grind against each other and cliffs are undermined, as the moving sand abrades and then moves on, the coast retreats. Over the great lengths of geologic time it may be worn back many, many miles. Even in the short length of historic time there are many examples of substantial changes.

Old maps of the Yorkshire coast of England show the locations of many towns that have long since been swept out of existence by the waves, their former sites now represented by sandbanks far out in the sea. In 1829 the famous geologist Charles Lyell reported a depth of twenty feet in the harbor at Sherringham where only forty-eight years before there had been a cliff fifty feet high with houses on it. Now the harbor too is gone. Near Cromer, also in England, the sea cliff has long been retreating at a rate of nineteen feet a year and at Covehithe and Southwold the erosion cuts the shore back ten to fifteen feet a year. During the great storm surge of 1953 (previously mentioned in connection with the Dutch dike failure) a cliff forty feet high at Suffolk retreated forty feet in a single night. A lower cliff lost ninety feet to the sea during the same night. Such extremely rapid erosion is the result of unusually violent waves brought to bear against unconsolidated materials by a water level too high for the beach to offer its usual protection. By contrast, careful examination of the hard rocks of the Cornish coast indicates that they probably have changed little over the last ten thousand years.

THE LONGSHORE TRANSPORT OF SAND

Most longshore currents are generated by waves striking the shoreline at an angle. Although wave fronts bend as they move across shallow water and tend to become parallel to the shore, often the re-

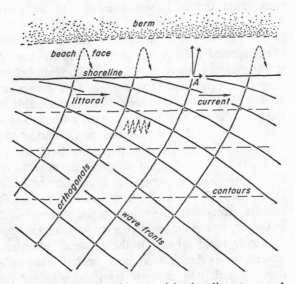

FIG. 69. Waves approaching a straight shoreline at an angle are not completely refracted. The remaining alongshore component (marked *A*) is responsible for the littoral current. Paths of sand grains moving to the right with every wave are shown by dotted lines.

fraction process is not quite complete. When the wave finally breaks at a slight angle, either on a bar or on the beach, the water receives an impulse, part

218

of which is in the alongshore direction. Therefore, the cumulative effect of many breaking waves is to move sand steadily alongshore.

Professor J. Munch-Petersen, who studied the Danish coast intensively for nearly forty years, drew the following analogy: "One can get a good picture of the material movement if one looks upon the wave as an excavating machine and the wave current as a conveyor belt that moves the material the machine has loosened. Each wave machine lifts the sand and impels it in a more or less oblique direction, adding it to the conveyor."

Over the years he modified the basic wave energy formula into one which he felt best described the ability of waves to transport material along a straight sandy coast:

$$\text{Material moved} = \frac{KH^2L \cos \alpha}{8}$$

in which alpha is the angle of wave attack and K is a coefficient that depends on the size of material and the steepness of the beach.

More recently Joseph Caldwell of the Beach Erosion Board established a relationship between the amount of alongshore energy and the amount of sand moved which gives similar results. It suggests that the energy expended in average weather to move the conveyor belt that extends from Point Conception to Los Angeles is roughly five million foot-pounds per foot of beach per day (or for one hundred miles, about fifty thousand horsepower).

Along that part of the California coast there is a delightful assortment of puzzling problems for the shoreline engineer, all created by an almost continuous littoral current from the west. This current is a product of the shape of the coast and the constant wave direction. North of Point Conception the coast faces due west, directly into the wind and waves. But south of the point the coast turns abruptly to the east so that the same winds and waves strike the shore at an angle. The current sweeps sand along the coast, and any structure that interrupts the flow acts like a dam, halting the flow of sand and causing the beaches to its west to grow. Beaches to the east of the structure are exposed to the inexorable waves

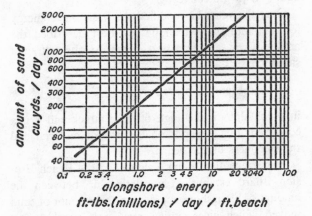

FIG. 70. The relationship between energy and alongshore transport. (after Caldwell, B.E.B.)

and currents, and without new sand constantly arriving they retreat rapidly.

The first major obstruction that the moving sand encounters is the Santa Barbara breakwater. As the sand moving along the beach from the west passes the tip of that structure, it abruptly encounters the deeper, quieter water that the breakwater was built to create. The wave-created turbulence that has held the sand in suspension ceases, and the particles are deposited just inside the end of the breakwater. But the filling in of the harbor is only half the problem. The beach to the east, deprived of its sand supply, is quickly stripped of sand and the soft cliffs behind are attacked. In the period 1938 to 1940 the Sand Point bluff was cut back one hundred to two hundred feet for over a mile. So, the solution for many years has been to dredge the sand from inside the breakwater and pump it into the first beach exposed to wave action, where it would remount the conveyor belt and continue on down the coast.

In the years 1948–50 the author made an extensive study of the sand motion in the Santa Barbara area for the University of California, under contract from the U. S. Corps of Engineers. The principal problem was to attempt to correlate the rate of sand motion with wind and wave action. We began by installing recording wind and wave meters at Santa Barbara and by making detailed beach profiles several miles upstream and downstream from the harbor. The principal areas of interest were, of course, the harbor itself and the first downstream berm. We soon discovered that the sand entering the harbor enlarged the perimeter of the sandspit in such a way that the growth was easy to measure. The new sand extended from low water down to the flat harbor bottom along its natural angle of repose. By making weekly surveys over a period of a year and plotting them as shown in Figure 71, we could then establish a relationship between the size of the waves and the growth of the spit. Since all the sand reaching Santa

Barbara went into the spit, the growth was a direct measurement of sand transport along that coast.

On days when the breaker height was less than two feet on the beach outside the breakwater, the spit grew at a rate of around two hundred and fifty cubic yards of sand a day; if the breakers were over four feet high, new sand moved in at one thousand cubic yards a day; and during storm conditions the rate

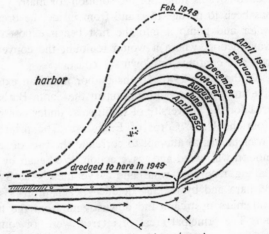

FIG. 71. Growth of the sandspit inside the end of the breakwater at Santa Barbara.

exceeded twenty-five hundred cubic yards a day. The average sand flow during the year and a half of our study was about six hundred cubic yards a day, but data accumulated by the U. S. Engineers over a period of years indicated long-term cyclic changes. Daily averages, obtained by dividing the amount of sand dredged out every two years by the number of intervening days, ranged from four hundred to nine hundred cubic yards. The highs and lows of these long-term variations appeared to come at about eleven-year intervals, and the author attempted without much success to correlate this rough periodicity with other natural phenomena. Doubtless it is related in some way to the position of the weather system that controls winds and waves in the Pacific. This, in turn, is probably connected with solar activity of an eleven-year period, but the mechanism that connects the two is not well understood.

Beyond Santa Barbara the moving sand encounters other obstacles, including the Ventura–Port Hueneme complex, which will be described presently. When the breakwater spit was dredged out every other year, great "waves" of sand would flow slowly down the coast; there were beaches that existed only on alternate years. Recently the fixed sand-pumping plant, first suggested by M. P. O'Brien in 1940, became part of the new plan of development.

The sand eventually reaches Santa Monica, much farther down the coast. That city also needed quiet water for a yacht harbor, but, aware of the sand problem and not wanting to become involved in never-ending dredging projects, it tried another solution. A breakwater was constructed parallel to the shore, several hundred yards out; the sand, it was hoped, would flow through the wide gap between breakwater and shore. It did not. Once in protected water, where the driving force of the waves ceased, the sand deposited. The result is that the beach behind the breakwater widens and itself becomes an obstruction to the movement of sand; downstream the beach retreats. So Santa Monica also uses a dredge to put the sand back into circulation.

The general mechanism of littoral drifting is apparent, but some of the details are obscure, so scientists are always seeking new ways of directly measuring the amount of sand suspended in the water and the depths at which it can be moved by various wave and current conditions. The use of radioactive sand for tracing the movement of beach material has been tried by scientists in Sweden, France, England, and the United States with some success. The idea is to take a sand with the proper kind of impurities (of the same size and physical properties as the sand on the beach to be studied) and expose it in a reactor until it becomes temporarily radioactive. Then the sand is placed on the beach and followed with Geiger counters. British experimenters used sand 0.18 mm in diameter activated with scandium 46, which has a half life of eighty-five days, and traced its motion for four months. They determined that only large storm waves would move sand at a depth of nineteen feet.

Similar experiments were then conducted with pebbles (shingle) on the east coast of England. The pebbles were taken from the beach to the nuclear laboratory at Harwell, where a radioactive coating was applied. The isotope used was barium 140–lanthanum 140, whose half life of twelve days made tracing of the pebbles possible for about six weeks.

Six hundred coated pebbles were dumped seven hundred yards offshore in water nineteen feet deep at low tide, and two thousand were placed in quite shallow water a dozen yards from the low tide shore. The positions of pebbles underwater were measured as often as weather conditions permitted—those off-shore with Geiger counters mounted on a sled towed along the sea bottom, those on the beach face with a scintillation counter. With these instruments it was possible to locate individual radioactive pebbles among the millions on the beach, even though they were buried as deep as nine inches.

During the observation period the pebbles in deeper water did not move at all, but those in shallow water spread out as much as a mile from their original position. For the first four weeks the weather was calm and wave heights never exceeded two feet. Even so, the ninety-three pebbles that were located had moved a mean distance of sixty yards. The next week the winds blew harder and from the opposite direction and the shingle migrated rapidly the other way. In so doing, some of the pebbles crossed a river mouth, apparently without being affected by the rapid tidal currents there. The researchers concluded that the movement of the shingle was directly related to the direction and strength of the winds blowing off the North Sea.

On the extreme Southern California coast Douglas Inman, of the Scripps Institution of Oceanography, has for years been studying the motion of sand in inshore waters. Spending much time on the bottom in diving gear, he has observed sand being raised by passing waves and moved by currents, has sampled the sand in suspension with various devices, and tried to establish the laws by which sand grains of various sizes respond to waves.

On the east coast, using one of the Beach Erosion Board model tanks, Thorndike Saville, Jr., set up an experiment to determine the amount of longshore transport under various wave conditions. Waves were generated that approached the shore at an angle of 10° in deep water and broke on a beach face that had an initial slope of 1:10. The velocity of the longshore current was obtained by timing the movement of dye and was found to increase with wave steepness. The moving sand was trapped and weighed at the downstream end and an equivalent amount introduced at the upstream end. In this manner the quantity of sand in motion could be carefully measured on what was, in effect, an endless beach.

By taking samples in four traps to measure transport in different zones, Saville was able to relate wave steepness to zone of transport. When wave steepness was less than 0.03, most of the sand moved by "beach drifting" in the swash zone on the beach face. Waves of greater steepness soon created a bar on which subsequent waves broke and raised the sand into suspension. From then on, the bulk of the transport occurred on the breaker zone along the bar. Others extended the experiments to include a greater range of direction of the approach of waves. It was then determined that when the wave front made an angle of 30° with the beach, the sand transport was maximum.

In similar experiments the British Hydraulics Research Board modeled a stretch of beach at Dunwich to determine the proper spacing of groins, a form of barrier we shall discuss further. By scaling from the model, they determined that on the open beach the sand transport was equal to 455,000 yards per year. If groins 180 feet long were spaced at intervals of 350 feet, this transport was reduced to 180,000 cubic yards per year. Although the experiment was not a realistic representation of actual conditions, the results do give the shoreline engineer a rough idea of the extent to which such barriers can be effective.

WHAT TO DO ABOUT LITTORAL DRIFT

The coastal engineer is constantly confronted with variations on the problem of how to keep sand moving along a shoreline and at the same time prevent the shore from eroding. If he builds any new shoreline facilities that stop the flow of sand, there will be trouble both at the place where the sand stops and the place where it would have gone. As with any problem posed by nature, the first step is to try to understand what is going on. If sand is filling a harbor, it is necessary to know where it comes from, how it is transported, and the rate at which it is arriving. If a beach is retreating, the engineer must know why before he can make plans to restore the sand. So he begins by making a study and obtaining answers to these critical questions. Then a plan of action must be developed and guided through the practical obstacle course that includes making legal, financial, and political arrangements, as well as the actual construction work.

Plans involving erosion-deposition problems inevitably rest on two solid pieces of knowledge: (1) Sand set in motion by wave-caused turbulence will settle out wherever a protective structure reduces wave action; (2) if no action is taken on erosion problems everyone shares the erosion, but as soon

227

as one part of the shore is protected the remainder
of the shore must supply the sand.

Usually the engineer's first question is: What is
the net littoral drift? How much sand will we have
to deal with in this problem?

The term "net littoral drift" refers to the difference between the volume of sand moving in one direction along a beach and that moving in the opposite
direction (caused by shifts in the direction of attack
of the waves). On a long, reasonably straight shoreline the net drift is of primary importance, and in
the Santa Barbara coast it is about 300,000 cubic
yards a year. But as Major General W. F. Cassidy
of the Corps of Engineers points out, where the moving sand must cross an inlet, the total amount of
sand in motion in both directions is important. He
cites figures for Corson Inlet, an unimproved inlet
through the barrier reef on the New Jersey coast:

Southward-moving sand	600,000 cu. yd/year
Northward-moving sand	450,000 cu. yd/year
Total sand moving	1,050,000 cu. yd/year
Net sand moving south	150,000 cu. yd/year

The total sand involved at the inlet is 1,050,000
cubic yards per year, which represents the amount
of sand that could be lost to the beach at that point.
In fact, the inlet historically removed 300,000 cubic
yards per year from the shore face although the net
littoral drift is only half of that. What happens? The
sand in shifting back and forth across the inlet is
moved out of the littoral conveyor area by transverse
tidal currents and is either carried out to sea, deposited as shoals in the channel, or is moved into the
bay behind. In any case, the result is erosion of the

beach, which must make up the deficiency by contributing the amount of sand withdrawn from the system. Moreover, the shift of the sand causes the inlet to migrate. If jetties were constructed to confine the flow of tidal water, at the end of a year there would be 150,000 cubic yards of sand accumulated north of the north jetty. This is the kind of situation in which it is worthwhile to think about installing a sand-transfer plant, with two objectives in mind: (1) to keep the entrance from shoaling, thus aiding navigation, and (2) to conserve 300,000 cubic yards of sand a year.

Such plants already exist in a number of places in the world, the best known at the Lake Worth Inlet, Florida, entrance to the port of Palm Beach. There a small sand-pumping plant on the updrift jetty picks up some of the sand that deposits there, pumps it through a pipeline, and discharges it on the downdrift side of the other jetty. Although this plant cannot handle all the drifting sand, it has stabilized the shoreline and, with the jetties, keeps the entrance free of shoals. It is at least the successful test of an idea. Every few years a special dredging operation moves the excess sand across the entrance and restores the balance.

There are places on the Southern California coast where such intermittent dredging has long been necessary. Clearly any new harbors or structures that interrupt the sand flow require either a fixed pumping plant or some sort of a plan for bypassing the interruption. At Port Hueneme, which is a few miles east of Santa Barbara and subject to the same littoral drifting, a harbor has been scooped in the flat coastal land and the entrance fenced with two parallel jetties, the westernmost of which stopped the sand. Periodically, as expected, it has been necessary to dredge the sand from this trap and dump it on the downdrift beaches. One difficulty is that the dredge must work under conditions that are rather hazardous for a floating pipeline dredge, exposed to the waves that move the sand. The need for enlarged harbor facilities in the area led Richard Eaton, chief technical adviser to the Beach Erosion Board, to propose a solution that seems to solve a series of problems simultaneously.

This new (Ventura County) harbor has been carved from the dunes immediately upstream of Port Hueneme and it too has parallel jetties, much like the first ones. But now the dredging situation is different, for a breakwater has been constructed parallel to the shore just west of the jetty; as at Santa Monica, this barrier causes the sand to deposit, but it also creates a zone of quiet water where a dredge can work without difficulty. Now, in one operation, the accumulated sand can be pumped around both harbor entrances and deposited on the beach beyond. This kind of sand-trapping, bypassing operation will doubtless come into more general use as the coast develops.

A similar but perhaps even more difficult problem has arisen sixty miles farther south, beyond the port of Los Angeles. The problem is that the natural sand supply for the beaches has been cut off. South and west of the Los Angeles plain the beaches in other years had been nourished with sand brought down from the hills by small intermittently-flowing streams. But in the last few decades the local need for water and the demand for flood control caused these "rivers" to be dammed and their channels lined with concrete. Now the sand is trapped in reservoirs well back from the ocean, and the starving beaches have steadily retreated, with erosion extending as far as Newport Beach. The littoral current strips an estimated 200,000 cubic yards of sand a year from the beaches and carries it south, eventually dumping it into the Newport submarine canyon, from which it cannot be retrieved.

When the erosion first became serious in 1947, a million cubic yards of sand were dredged from the Anaheim Bay channel and deposited on the beaches to widen them. By 1963 the continuing attrition had made the situation on some of the beaches critical again—seventy-five houses were smashed by waves in a single storm. So another three million yards will be dredged from Anaheim Bay and dumped on the upstream beaches. The littoral drift will carry it along the shore toward Newport, a wave of sand that widens the beaches as it advances. But there is a limit to how much sand is available in the nearby bays and entrances. Now the plan is to arrest the flow of sand just before it reaches the canyon; a breakwater twenty-six hundred feet long is to be built parallel to the shore much like those at Santa Monica and Ventura. Then, about every five years this stockpile can be dredged up and pumped back to the point of beginning, thus insuring a long life for the valuable beach property.

THE EFFECT OF GROINS

For many years the accepted method of dealing with shoreline erosion problems was to build groins. A groin is a dam-like structure, usually a few feet high and about a hundred feet long, constructed perpendicular to the shoreline. Its objective is to retard the loss of a beach, widening it by trapping the passing sand. Groins may be made of timber, sheet-steel pilings, stone, or concrete. Some are built solid, to be impervious to sand flow; others—permeable groins—are constructed with openings that permit appreciable quantities of sand to flow through. Ordinarily a system of groins is built to protect a long section of shoreline. Some parts of the New York and New Jersey coasts have "groin fields" extending for many miles. As material accumulates on the updrift side and the beach there widens, the supply of sand to the downdrift side is correspondingly reduced and the beach retreats. So, the solution is to build another groin, and another, and another. The slope of the beach face on the updrift side progressively steepens while that on the downdrift side flattens. Often the updrift side fills and overflows, the swashes of high tide carrying the sand over the top and spilling it on the low side, and soon a system of groins produces a series of short curving beaches that give the shoreline the cuspate appearance shown in the accompanying drawing. As each groin fills, the sand bypasses the end and proceeds down the coast.

Although properly engineered groins can capture and retain sand, their effect is usually local and temporary. Persons with beach-front property in imminent danger of being washed away are understandably eager to take fast action, and without investigation they may build a groin in the hope of restoring their beach. But there may not be any sand passing, or the groin may be built in the wrong place and actually accelerate the erosion. The motion of coastal sand is more complex than one might suppose.

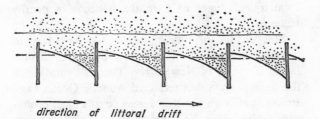

direction of littoral drift

FIG. 72. Groins are low dams intended to arrest the sand moving alongshore in the hope of maintaining or widening the original (dashed line) shoreline.

Sometimes groins are helpful. There is an instance in which a ship saved a lighthouse, instead of vice versa. In 1883 the Cape Henlopen light on the Delaware coast was in imminent danger of being undermined by the sea. The high-water mark reached around the base and various emergency protective actions were being considered. Then in a storm the *Minnie Hunter* was driven ashore, grounding about five hundred feet north of the lighthouse. The wrecked ship immediately acted as a groin which dammed the coastal flow of sand and replaced the beach in front of the light so that the structure survived for many more years.

Because groins rarely give a satisfactory long-term solution they are no longer the preferred means of maintaining a beach. In the long run they are usually more expensive and less effective than a "beach nourishment" program. Now the fashion is to add more sand, as in the Newport Beach area. Even the famous Waikiki Beach in Honolulu is periodically rebuilt with sand trucked in from dunes fourteen miles away. In other programs new sand is supplied to the "headwaters" of the littoral stream from inland dunes or from the bottoms of nearby lagoons.

This change of opinion about the best way to maintain beaches is illustrated by the problem now facing the state of New Jersey. The configuration of the coast is such that refracted Atlantic Ocean swell strikes heavily on the New Jersey coast's most prominent point, near Barnegat Inlet. Littoral currents move the sand away from the point in both directions, and the point is eroding rapidly. In the past fifty years nearly $50 million has been spent on shore works in an attempt to stabilize the shoreline. The present annual rate of expenditure is more than $2 million, and the results are not entirely satisfactory. Some parts of the shore have long since been stripped of sand; others are still retreating. In several places elaborate groin systems have failed.

The Beach Erosion Board studied the New Jersey problem and proposed a project to develop adequate recreational beaches and prevent further erosion. This project will nourish all the beaches along the coast by supplying new sand to the beaches in the vicinity of Barnegat Inlet. The sand will come partly by truck from inland locations and partly by pumping from Barnegat Bay; wave action and littoral currents can be relied upon to distribute it along the coast. The estimated initial investment is $28 million, but the program will require less than $1 million per year to maintain the beaches thereafter.

Sixty-six other shoreline construction projects, costing a total of over $100 million, have been planned for the shores of the United States and about half are completed or are well under way. Beach erosion is a problem of increasing importance as coastal land is developed intensively.

Chapter XI

MAN AGAINST THE SEA

The sea can be either friendly or hostile. It is calm and beautiful one day, furious and terrifying the next. On days calm enough to make surveys and do construction work one must not forget that before long unleashed violence will follow. The destructive power of the sea against ships and beaches has been described. Now we will consider what happens when waves smash against harbor defenses and shoreline installations, and what can be done to withstand the onslaught.

The solution to any problem begins with the attempt to understand what is going on. What is the nature of the forces? How do they act? What levels of energy are involved?

Previous chapters contain background information about the various kinds of waves, the way in which they refract as they enter shoal water and the manner in which they are transformed into breakers. Now we must make use of this information in the design of coastal works that defend against the sea's attack. Experience is a good, although perhaps a hard, teacher, and it is well to begin by recalling some instances in which violent wave action has damaged shoreline structures in the past. These serve as a warning—reminding us of the extreme forces which waves may exert once in a decade or a century. Then we will consider various means that can be used to defend our shores and harbors against the worst the sea can do.

WAVES ATTACK

Case histories of wave attack on man's coastal structures make fascinating reading, for this aspect of the lore of the sea makes its great power most apparent. Many of the following examples were collected by D. D. Gaillard and presented in *Wave Action in Relation to Engineering Structure*, published nearly sixty years ago. Lighthouses, by the very concept, are natural recipients of violent wave action since they often are built on rocky headlands or submarine ledges to keep ships at a safe distance. Some of them are called "wave-swept towers," and it is understandable that lighthouse keepers should be an endless source of stories about fabulous waves and marine disasters.

For example: During the construction of the Dhu Heartach lighthouse in 1872, fourteen stones of ten tons weight each, which had been fixed into the tower by joggles and Portland cement at the level of thirty-seven feet above high water, were torn out and carried into deep water.

A door in the Unst light, 195 feet above the sea, was once broken open by the impact of flying water, and windows in the Dunnet Head light station in north Scotland, 300 feet above the water, are sometimes broken by rocks flung up by the waves.

In 1923 the St. George Reef lighthouse near Crescent City, California, experienced a storm in which breaking waves swept over the foundation platform of the lighthouse tower, seventy feet above the water, tearing a donkey engine from its foundation.

At Trinidad Head, California, a few miles to the south, the light is set on a rocky promontory 195 feet above mean sea level, which doubtless seemed to its designers like a good safe height. This illusion was shattered in 1913 when the lightkeeper reported: "At 4:40 PM I observed a wave of unusual height. When it struck the bluff, the jar was heavy. The lens immediately stopped revolving. The sea shot up the face of the bluff and over it, until solid sea seemed to me to be on a level with where I stood by the lantern."

Several lighthouses are famous for having been swept away entirely by great storms and having been replaced more than once. These include the Eddystone light, Bishop's Rock light, and the original Minot's Ledge light, off the Massachusetts coast, which was destroyed several times during construction and in 1851 crumpled into the sea carrying its two lightkeepers with it. In the midst of a great storm people on the main coast heard the frantic ringing of its bell abruptly terminate. Little evidence could be found afterward that a lighthouse had ever stood there. The new stone shaft that replaced it rises ninety-seven feet directly from the sea, has now stood for over one hundred years, and the U. S. Coast Guard is proud that waves often sweep over the entire structure causing no effect except strong vibration.

Of all the stories, those about the light on Tilla-mook Rock, a few miles south of the Columbia River mouth, are retold most often. The rock itself, several miles at sea, has nearly vertical walls rising to a ragged surface about ninety feet above MLLW on which the lighthouse was built. During every se-vere storm the entire rock shudders and fragments torn from the base of the cliff are thrown on top of the rock. In a December storm a rock weighing 135 pounds was thrown higher than the light, which is 139 feet above the sea, and in falling back broke a hole twenty feet square in the roof of the light-keeper's house, practically wrecking the interior of the building. On another occasion a fragment of rock weighing about half a ton was rolled across the plat-form at the base of the building, ninety-one feet above low water, smashing a wrought-iron fence. In 1902 a keeper reported that water was thrown to a height of fully two hundred feet above the level of the sea, "descending in apparently solid water on the roof." Ten years later another keeper, investigating trouble with the foghorn (ninety-five feet above the water) found it filled with small rocks. After the glass of the lantern was broken on several occasions by rocks, a heavy steel grating was installed 135 feet above the sea, just below the lens, to prevent further damage.

As a result of this process of trial and error, which now extends over two thousand years, increasingly heavy construction has been used, and the problem of maintaining lighthouses on exposed rocks seems to have been reasonably well solved—except in such special cases as the Scotch Cap light described in Chapter VI.

The only stories about wave violence that can top the lighthouse accounts are those about breakwaters. At Cherbourg, France, the breakwater was built as an immense embankment of loose stone protected in places by 700-cubic-foot concrete blocks. A wall twenty feet high surmounts the stone embankment. During a severe storm on Christmas Day many years ago stones weighing seven thousand pounds were thrown over the top of the wall and many of the concrete blocks moved as much as sixty feet.

In the Shetland Islands a block of stone weighing five and a half tons was detached from its bed situated seventy-two feet above the high tide level and moved more than twenty feet. Another block weighing eight tons was torn up and driven by the waves over several ledges with vertical faces two to seven feet high for a distance of seventy feet at an average level of twenty feet above high water.

In an especially severe gale at Buffalo, New York, in December 1899, considerable damage was inflicted by waves upon timber-crib breakwater which had been completed but a few weeks previously. This gale was of unusual violence, the wind blowing at times at the rate of eighty miles per hour from the west. The water level of the lake varied from 3 feet below mean lake level to 6.4 feet above the same datum between 4 PM and midnight. Tremendous seas broke over the breakwater. The waves, dashing against the vertical walls of the structure, rose to a great height above it, variously estimated at from 75 to 125 feet, enveloping the breakwater in an immense sheet of water. In falling, the water struck the top of the superstructure with such force as to crush the large timbers of which it was constructed. Be-

cause the direction of the breakwater was at right
angles to the axis of the storm, the destructive power
of the furious waves was accentuated. Seventy 12-
by-12 inch timbers, ten feet between supports and
spaced five feet from center to center, were broken
in the middle by the impact of the falling water.
About nine hundred feet of superstructure in all was
smashed almost to the water's edge.

The breakwater at Wick Bay in Scotland often
faces into violent waves, and its failure in 1872
was described by Thomas Stevenson in *The Construction of Harbours*: "The end of the breakwater
was composed of three courses of blocks weighing
80 to 100 tons each which were deposited as a foundation in a trench made in cement rubble. Above
this foundation there were three courses of large
stones carefully set in cement, and the whole was
surmounted by a large monolith of cement rubble,
measuring about 26 by 45 feet by 11 feet in thickness, weighing upward of 800 tons. As a further
precaution, iron rods 3.5 inches in diameter were
fixed in the uppermost of the foundation courses of
cement rubble. These rods were carried through the
courses of stonework by holes cut in the stone, and
were finally embedded in the monolithic mass, which
formed the upper portion of the pier.

"Incredible as it may seem, this huge mass suc-
cumbed to the force of the waves, and Mr. Mc-
Donald, the resident engineer, actually watched from
the adjacent cliff as it was gradually slewed round
by successive strokes until it was finally removed and
deposited inside the pier. It was several days before
an examination could be made of this singular phenomenon, but the result of the examination only

gave rise to increased amazement at the feat which the waves had actually achieved. Divers found that the 800-ton monolith forming the upper portion of the pier, which the resident engineer had seen in the act of being washed away, had carried with it the whole of the lower courses, which were attached to it by the iron bolts, and that this enormous mass, weighing not less than 1350 tons, had been removed in one piece and was resting on the rubble at the side of the pier, having sustained no damage but a slight fracture at the edges. The second course of cement blocks, on which the 1350-ton mass rested, had been swept off after being relieved of the superincumbent weight, and some of the blocks were found entire near the head of the breakwater. The removal of this protection left the end of the breakwater exposed and the storm, which continued to rage for some days after the destruction of the cement rubble defense, carried away about 150 feet of the masonry (one-seventh of the whole)."

The structure was rebuilt and a much larger cap was added, this one weighing 2600 tons, but five years later another storm treated it quite as roughly. There is no record of whether Mr. McDonald kept his job and made a third attempt. Captain D. D. Gaillard, U.S.A., later computed that the wave forces required to move the second cap must have been 6340 pounds per square foot.

In November 1950 extraordinary waves from a storm on Lake Michigan moved a concrete cap on the U. S. Steel Company's breakwater at Gary, Indiana. This cap, 200 feet long and weighing 2600 tons, moved three to four feet laterally when pounded by 7.2 second waves about fourteen feet high. Knowing the mass of the concrete, to motion, the engineers computed that the wave pressure required to move the cap must have been between 1440 and 2500 pounds per square foot—or 1680 tons of nearly instantaneous wave pressure.

MAN DEFENDS

The words that Captain Gaillard wrote more than sixty years ago to describe the effects of waves on structures are as valid as ever: "If wave motion is arrested by any interposing barrier, a part at least of the energy of the wave will be exerted against the barrier itself, and unless the latter is strong enough to resist the successive attacks of the waves, its destruction will ensue.

"No other force of equal intensity so severely tries every part of the structure against which it is exerted, and so unerringly detects each weak place or faulty detail of construction.

"The reason for this is found in the diversity of ways in which the wave force may be exerted and transmitted; for example: (1) The force may be a static pressure due to the head of a column of water; or (2) it may result from the kinetic effect of rapidly moving particles of the fluid; or (3) from the impact of a body floating upon the surface of the water and hurled by the wave against the structure; or (4) the rapid subsidence of the mass of water thrown against a structure may produce a partial vacuum, causing sudden pressures to be exerted from within.

"These effects may be transmitted through joints or cracks in the structure itself; (a) by hydraulic pressure, or (b) pneumatic pressure, or by a combination of the two; or (c) the shock produced by the impact of the waves may be transmitted as vibrations through the materials of which the structure is composed."

In order to design any kind of structure that will stand against wave action, one must have numbers that describe the amounts of energy involved and the magnitude of the forces imposed.

The energy in a wave is equally divided between potential energy and kinetic energy. The potential energy, resulting from the elevation or depression of the water surface, advances with the wave form; the kinetic energy is a summation of the motion of the particle in the wave train and advances with the group velocity (in shallow water this is equal to the wave velocity).

The amount of energy in a wave is the product of the wave length and the *square* of the wave height, as follows:

$$E = \frac{wLH^2}{8}$$

where w is the weight of a cubic foot of water (64 pounds).

Thus we can compare the energy in three waves of ten-second period, one 4 feet high, one 8 feet high, and one 12 feet high. The four-foot wave contains 65,600 foot-pounds of energy (per foot of wave crest) or 33 foot-tons; the eight-foot wave has 131 foot-tons, and the twelve-foot wave 295 foot-tons. A big difference! For practical purposes the deep-water formula applies to shallow-water waves.

The question of exactly how much pressure large

waves exert against structures was investigated by
Thomas Stevenson, beginning in 1842. He invented
a simple, rugged dynamometer and made the first
measurements of wave force. The instrument con-
sisted merely of a plate six inches in diameter facing
into the waves, mounted on a stiff horizontal spring.
Behind the spring was a rod held by a friction grip
in such a fashion that it would move as the plate
moved but remain at the maximum distance to
which the plate pushed it. As each increasingly large
wave impacted against the plate, the rod would be
pushed to a new position. The distance moved times
the spring constant gave the maximum wave force
exerted on the plate during the storm.

He reported that at Skerryvore Rocks in the Atlantic the maximum force of waves in a storm which
had an average height of ten feet was 3041 pounds
per square foot (psf), for twenty-foot swell 4502
psf, and for strong gales with waves in excess of
twenty feet, 6083 psf.

The disadvantage of this type of instrument is that
it registers only the dynamic pressure of moving
water and ignores the hydrostatic pressure; moreover, there is only a single maximum reading per
storm. Years later Captain Gaillard decided to build
a diaphragm type of dynamometer that would measure total force and use it to probe the pressure of
wave impact in more detail. After using the new instrument for a while he worked out a formula for the
maximum pressure exerted by a breaking wave:

$$\text{Pressure} = 1.31 \ (C+V)^2 \frac{\rho}{2g}$$

in which C is the wave velocity, V is the maximum

orbital velocity at the crest of the wave, and ρ is the mass density of water. For a wave ten feet high with a period of five seconds, a typical Great Lakes storm wave, the pressure calculated from Gaillard's formula is 1240 pounds per square foot, which agrees well with the 1210 psf registered by his instrument. By installing a series of dynamometers at various heights above and below the average water level he found that for breaking waves the pressure increases with the height above the trough, reaching a maximum of about half the breaker's height (roughly the still-water level at that moment).

More recently R. R. Minikin, a British engineer, has established a different series of relationships between wave pressures, thrust against structures and overturning moments, but these give approximately equivalent answers. Now, armed with modern crystal pressure transducers, electronic amplifiers and continuously recording apparatus, the store of data is rapidly increasing, and the results can be examined statistically. The highest wave-pressure measurement on record was taken at Dieppe, France, in 1938, where A. de Rouvelle reported instantaneous pressures of 12,700 psf (the pressure above 6000 psf lasted only for 1/100 of a second).

THE DESIGN OF SHORELINE STRUCTURES

There are four major kinds of shoreline structures: jetties, breakwaters, seawalls, and dikes. All are made usually of some combination of rock and concrete. Jetties, usually in pairs, extend into the ocean at river entrances or bay mouths to confine the flow of water to a narrow zone. If concentrated between a pair of jetties, the ebb and flow of tidal water keeps the sand in motion and prevents shoaling in the channel. A breakwater is a structure that protects a shore area, harbor, or anchorage from wave action. Often it is built well out from shore to provide a substantial area of quiet water. A seawall is built at the shoreline separating land from water. It is the man-made equivalent of a rocky cliff, designed to protect softer material from erosion. A dike is a special form of impermeable breakwater that acts as a dam. When the zone it protects is pumped dry, it becomes a special kind of seawall.

What can the engineer do to insure that such structures survive against wave attack? He has several choices which he tries to combine into the most efficient solution. He can carefully locate the structure so that its position and shape and orientation give it the most favorable chance for survival; he can build in such a fashion that wave energy is reflected or absorbed; he can build with large and dense materials, simply resisting the wave forces with weight. Always, he considers all factors that enter into the various possibilities and tries to optimize his solution. The final plan is not necessarily the best possible structure to resist waves but the best thing that can be done considering cost, time, use of existing facilities, kind of rock that is available, probable increase in the use of the installation, and, of course, political influences of many kinds. The engineer must fight as hard as he can for the best solution, but he is overruled often and ends up building a structure of which he may not wholeheartedly approve.

Here we will review only the technical areas

within which the designer can maneuver to obtain the best engineering solution. No matter what other factors may ultimately influence the decision on what is to be constructed, this is always the first step.

The location of the structure comes first. For breakwaters the underwater topography and the refraction conditions usually influence the design most. In Chapter IV the process of making statistical studies of waves and drawing refraction diagrams was described. Briefly, the idea is to obtain as much information as possible about the waves arriving at the proposed harbor by hindcasting from old weather charts. The charts will give the dominant wave direction and period as well as the probable height of the largest or most damaging waves. Then refraction diagrams are prepared; these are basic design data for the breakwater builder. Now taking into consideration the underwater topography, the general configuration of the coast, and the proposed locations of piers and wharves, the engineer can lay out various breakwater locations. Probably he will not want the structure to be exactly parallel to the wave fronts from the most probable direction. If it were, a wave could impact along the whole length of the structure at the same instant. Usually he will spread the stress out by presenting an angular front to the worse seas. Perhaps he will make model tests, first in a ripple tank, then in a larger wave tank.

In locating jetty pairs, which often are parallel rocky structures extending directly into the ocean, a major problem is to space them properly so that the velocity of the moving tidal water will be sufficiently high to scour the sand from the entrance channel and keep it deep enough for ship traffic. If the distance between them is too great, the water will flow at lower velocity, and its energy will be diffused so that the channels will be shallow and sandbars will obstruct the entrance. On the other hand, if the jetties are too close together the currents are likely to scour the sand from beneath the stones and undermine them. One can get an idea of the proper spacing by studying the natural channels. In the late 1930s M. P. O'Brien examined a number of bays along the U.S. Pacific coast and determined that a constant ratio exists between the area of the entrance

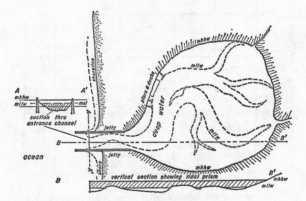

FIG. 73. Bay harbor showing tidal prism (the volume of water between mean higher high water and mean lower low water).

section and the volume of the tidal prism. The tidal prism is the volume of water inside a bay or harbor that is enclosed by planes of mean higher high water and mean lower low water. In other words, it is the average volume of water that flows in and out during a 12.4-hour tidal cycle. Shoreline engineers who disregard this fundamental design law and arbitrarily space jetties at a greater distance than indicated by Figure 74 can look forward to years of dredging to keep open a channel that could be maintained by natural forces.

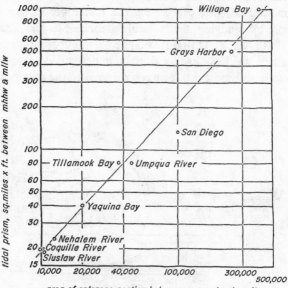

FIG. 74. Relationship between tidal prism and entrance section. (after O'Brien)

The next problem of the design engineer is to devise a shape for the structure that will reflect, absorb, or otherwise cushion the effects of large waves. It is possible to get rid of some of the wave energy by reflecting it; this approach may or may not be helpful, depending on the circumstances. If the structure

in question rises almost vertically from water too
deep for the waves to break, the wave can be reflected back to sea with little loss of energy. But few
breakwaters are designed to reflect more than a small
part of the energy. More often they absorb the wave
with rough faces of rock. Seawalls, on the other hand,
usually are designed to reflect a substantial part of
the wave energy that reaches them. Often they have
a series of steps, each about two feet high, from
which the water reflects without loading the whole
structure simultaneously. Others have an overhang-
ing recurved surface which has the effect of throwing
the landward-rushing water seaward, back upon itself. But if the face of the seawall curves so as to
guide the water straight upward, as some old designs
did, the water will fall back on the wall with great
force, possibly damaging it and eroding the land it
is intended to protect. A properly-designed wave re-
flector has the effect of starting a new wave moving
seaward which tends to cancel the next oncoming
wave it encounters, or at least reduce its force.

The resistance of rocks in a shoreline structure
such as a breakwater or jetty to overturning or sliding is obviously of great interest to the shore-pro-
tection engineer. Dense rock is far more useful, as
the following example shows. Compare a block of
granite five feet on each side (125 cubic feet) with
a block of sandstone the same size. The granite
weighs 170 pounds per cubic foot in air (106 underwater) and the sandstone 140 pounds per cubic
foot (76 underwater). The force required to over-
turn the granite is 540 pounds per square foot of
wave pressure, but the sandstone goes over at 390
pounds per square foot. Therefore the largest, densest

rocks make the best breakwater material. Moreover, a line of properly placed or connected rocks
tend to support each other and can resist more pressure than isolated blocks.

For some reason rectangular artificial blocks are
nearly always less stable than randomly-shaped
natural rocks of the same unit weight used under the
same conditions. This curious fact, long observed
and eventually confirmed by systematic experiments, constituted a real challenge to engineers. The
question to be answered was: What is the best shape
for an artificial protecting block? Pierre Daniel and
others at the Neyrpic Hydraulics Laboratory at Grenoble, France, began by setting down the properties that the new blocks—of whatever shape—should
have. They decided these should be permeable so
that the water could freely flow through. This solution would avoid creating any internal or back pressure (which at the Mers-el-Kebir naval base had
bodily lifted a revetment composed of 400-ton
blocks); it would reduce overtopping and reflection.
The block should be shaped so as to have few
plane surfaces; in fact, it should be as rough as possible to dissipate wave energy in turbulence; it should
have maximum resistance. Combinations of blocks
should interlock so that they could mutually support
each other.

After many preliminary tests a sort of sea monster
with four tentacles was patented under the name of
"tetrapod." The most suitable proportions between
legs and body were worked out with due consideration for the problem of manufacture, and not long
afterward tetrapods began to appear in shoreline
structures. They are most useful when placed in a

double outer layer facing the worst wave action over a core of natural stone and rubble.

By bringing to bear all the factors mentioned here, successful shoreline structures can be designed. From

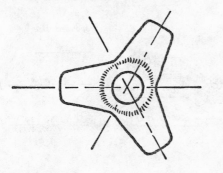

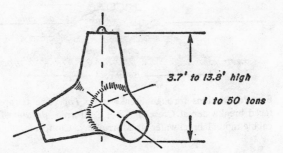

3.7' to 13.8' high

1 to 50 tons

FIG. 75. Tetrapods: four-legged sea monsters of concrete used for breakwater facing.

the outside, to the uninitiated, the seawall may look like a rather ordinary piece of concrete with steps built for the convenience of bathers. Or the breakwater may look like a carelessly-dumped pile of rock instead of carefully built-up layers. The accompanying figures (76 and 77) show the physical foundations and inner cores of several kinds of structures, but they do not show the true foundation—the years

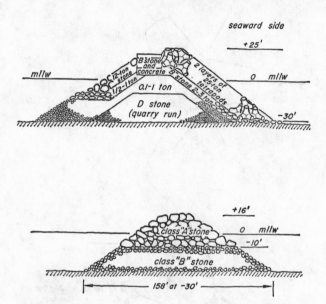

FIG. 76. Sections through breakwaters. *Top:* The tetrapod-faced breakwater at Crescent City, California. *Bottom:* The rubble-mound breakwater at Morro Bay, California.

of hard-won experience and the elaborate computations that went into the design. A subject so complicated has many variations depending on local conditions and requirements, and this chapter obviously can do no more than give a hasty survey. If any reader has been stimulated to look further, I

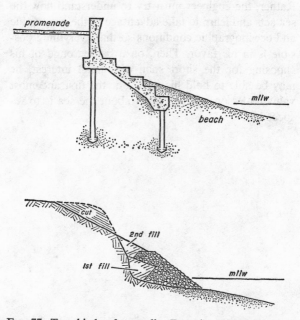

Fig. 77. Two kinds of seawalls. *Top:* A concrete-step sea-wall with a re-entrant curved section, resting on sheet piling driven deep into the beach. *Bottom:* A soft cliff is graded to a new slope and protected by a rubble-mound wall.

can recommend the *Proceedings of the Conferences on Coastal Engineering*, edited by J. W. Johnson and Robert Wiegel, of the Council on Wave Research.

* * *

The ocean is huge, powerful, and eternal. Puny man can scarcely expect to win by overwhelming it, and anyone who counters its attack with brute-force solutions is doomed to expensive disappointment.

Rather, the engineer must try to understand how the sea acts and learn to take advantage of the geographic and oceanographic conditions so that everything possible is in his favor. Then, on a battleground of his choosing for the short span of human interest, he may be able to hold his own. For the first and most valuable lesson one can learn about the sea is to respect it.

EPILOGUE

Many of the pleasantest hours of the author's life have been spent in watching waves and examining beaches, trying to understand them. Walking and meditating, photographing, digging and surveying—the curious quest, already in progress for over sixteen years, has been great fun in spite of uncounted salt-water drenchings and numerous scientific disappointments. It has covered thousands of miles of shoreline in a dozen countries without losing any of its fascination, and without producing any hope of complete understanding. The subject is too complex. But somehow there is satisfaction in being aware enough of the ways of waves and beaches to detect the special softness of a new layer of sand underfoot that means the berm is building or to observe a slight change in the appearance of the breakers and think, "There must be a new storm in the Gulf of Alaska."

The inner peace that comes with the quiet contemplation of a beach on a still calm morning, or the feeling of exhilaration that comes from riding a great wave in a small boat, is more reward than most men ever know. Fortunately the beaches of the world are cleaned every night by the tide. A fresh look always awaits the student, and every wave is a masterpiece of originality.

It will ever be so. Go and see.

ADDITIONAL READING

DEFANT, ALBERT. *Ebb and Flow*. University of Michigan Press, Ann Arbor, 1958. 121 pages.

RUSSELL, R. C. H., AND D. H. MACMILLAN. *Waves and Tides*. Philosophical Library, New York, 1953. 348 pages.

Popular but more detailed accounts of the nature of waves and tides than are given here.

KING, C. A. M. *Beaches and Coasts*. St. Martin's Press, New York, 1960. 403 pages.

SHEPARD, F. P. *Submarine Geology*. Harper and Brothers, New York, 1948. 348 pages.

Texts that deal with beaches and other coastal and underwater features in a comprehensive way that is not difficult to read.

MINIKIN, R. C. R. *Winds, Waves and Maritime Structures*. Charles Griffin and Company, London, 1950. 216 pages.

Shore Protection Planning and Design, Beach Erosion Board, Corps of Engineers Technical Report No. 4. U. S. Government Printing Office, Washington, D. C., 1961. 300 pages.

These are concerned with the engineering problems of design and construction of breakwaters, groins, jetties, and shoreline structures. The language is necessarily technical, but there are many illustrations as well as useful tables, graphs, and explanations.

The various publications of the Council on Wave Research are recommended as a means of keeping abreast of new developments in wave research and shoreline engineering. Address: University of California Field Station, Richmond, California.

INDEX

Airy, Sir George, 30, 39, 94

Alaska coast, 92; rise of, 11–12; tsunamis on, 111, 116–17

Amazon bore, 95

Antarctic Ocean, tides of, 92

Atlantic coast of North America: barrier islands of, 20–22; beaches of, 184–85, 194, 196; erosion of, 12, 214, 232–35; New York harbor, 17–20; tides of, 88–89, 91–92; storm waves on, 81, 238

Backrush, 204–7

Bagnold, R. A., 198

Baja (Lower) California, 14, 185

Barrier islands, 20–22

Bars: defined, 22, 188, 200; effect on waves of, 200–3; formation of, 16–20, 190–92; number per beach of, 202–3; rip currents and, 170–73; slope of beaches and, 193–97

Bays: seiches in, 97–101; tidal bores in, 93–95; tidal prisms of, 249–50. *See*

also Surging

Bazin, Henri, 30

Beach face: defined, 23; size of sand and slope of, 199–200

Beaches, 184–212; berms *vs.* bars in, 22–23; composition of, 14, 184–87; cusps on, 207–10; defined, 13–15; domes and pinholes on, 210–11; first formation of, 6; formation of, 15–22; low-tide step on, 207; ripple marks and, 211–12; slope of, 193–97, 199–201; uprush and backrush on, 204–7; in winter *vs.* summer, 23, 188–92, 197–98. *See also* Bars; Berms; Erosion of shoreline; Sand; Surf; Surf zone

Beaufort scale, 48–49

Bengal, Bay of, storm surges in, 79–81

Berms: defined, 22, 188; wave height and, 198–99; in winter *vs.* summer, 188–92, 197–98. *See also* Beaches

261

Bernoulli contour system, 122, 124

Bolin, Rolf, 110

Breaking waves, 54–55; bars and, 201–2; force of, 148; oil and, 61; in surf, 159–65; surf beat and, 166–67; in tsunamis, 109–11

Breakwaters: breaking waves and, 68; defined, 247; design of, 248, 251–54; destroyed by waves, 74–77, 240–43; sand motion and, 220–24

Caldwell, Joseph, 219, 220

California coast: beaches of, 15, 184–85, 193–201; erosion of, 213, 230–31; littoral transport of sand on, 219–23, 229–31; rise of, 12; surging on, 100–1; tidal currents on, 92; tsunami on, 109–10; wave refraction at Long Beach, 74–77

Canals, surfing of barges on, 128

Cannes, France, beach at, 185

Carmel, Calif., beach at, 195, 197–98

Cassidy, Maj. Gen. W. F., 228

China, tidal bores in, 94–95

Choppy sea: defined, 43; periods of, 9

Clapotis, 68

Coasts: defined, 14; rise and fall of, 11–13. *See also* Beaches; Erosion of shoreline; *specific coasts*

Continental shelves, 6; seiches and, 99; slope of, 7

Continents: formation of, 4–5; rise and fall of, 11–13

Cornish, Vaughan, 30, 57, 63

Cusps, 207–10

Daniel, Pierre, 252

"Dead water," 125–26

Dikes: defined, 247; of Holland, in storm surge (1953), 78–79

"Drowned topography," 12

Diffraction of waves, 69–70

Domes on beaches, 210–11

Dukws, 127, 174–82

Earth: geological processes of, 4–6. *See also* Continents; Tides

Earthquake waves. *See* Tsunamis

Eaton, Richard, 230

Eckart, Carl, 137

Eckman, V. W., 125

Energy of waves, 243–46; energy spectra describing waves, 50–53; equation for, 244; in littoral transport of sand, 219, 220; in swell, 65

English coast, 14; beaches of, 185; erosion of, 214, 217; Severn bore, 94

Erosion of shoreline, 213–17; groins and, 232–35; littoral drift and, 227–31; by storms, 197–98

Estuaries: tides in, 91, 93–95. *See also* Bays

European coast, 20; beaches of, 185, 193, 196; storm surge (1955) on, 78–79. *See also* English coast

Explosion-generated waves, 117–21

Fetch: defined, 44; length of, in fully developed seas, 53

Foamlines (waves of translation), 69, 161, 167; force of, 148; theory of, 164–65

Fully developed seas, 9, 44–45, 51

Gaillard, Capt. D. D., 30, 237, 242, 243, 245

Galileo, 83

Galveston, Tex., "flood," 78

Gerstner, Franz, 27–28, 30, 39

Groins, 232–35

Gulf coast of U.S.: barrier islands of, 20; storm surges on, 78

"Gunk" in experimentation, 37, 39–41

Half Moon Bay, Calif.: beach at, 200–1; tsunami at, 109–10

Hall effect, 125

Harbors. *See* Bays; *specific harbors*

Hawaii: beaches of, 195, 197, 234; erosion in, 234; tsunamis at, 110–16

Headlands, beaches and, 200–1

Heck, N. H., 106

Henwood, J. W., 215

Holland: storm surge (1953) onto, 78–79

Hurricanes. *See* Storm surges; Storms

Ice, wave height and, 61

Indian Ocean: storm surges in, 79–81; tides in, 89, 92

Inman, Douglas, 225

Instruments for wave measurement, 131–49; for tsunami warning, 112–15; for wave force, 146–49, 245–46

Issacs, John, 145, 167, 174

James, R. W., 31, 51

Japanese beaches, 193, 196

Jeffries, Sir Harold, 31

Jetties: defined, 246–47; location of, 248–50

Johnson, J. W., 190, 255

Kelp, wave height and, 61–62

Kelvin, Lord, 122, 133, 137

Kepler, Johannes, 83

Knot, defined, 51

Krakatoa volcano, 117–19

Lake Worth Inlet, Fla., 229

Lakes: storms on, 240–41, 242–43. *See also* Seiches

Lamb, Horace, 31

Leadbetter Spit, Wash., 193, 196, 203

Lewis, E. V., 155

Lighthouses: destruction of, 111, 237–39; erosion and, 214

Littoral transport of sand, 213, 218–31; engineering problems of, 227–31

Los Angeles, Calif., harbor: surging at, 101; wave refraction at, 74–77

Lower (Baja) California, 14, 185

Lyell, Charles, 217

Margraff, Lieut. F. C., 59

Marks, Wilbur, 157

Mass transport in waves, 38–40

Minikin, R. R., 246

MLLW, defined, 202

Moon and tides, 83–88

Moore, Cmdr. W. U., 94

Munch-Petersen, J., 219

Munk, Walter H., 8–9, 31, 45, 112–13, 132, 167

Net littoral drift, defined, 228

Neumann, G., 31, 50, 51

New England coast, 12; storm surges on, 81

New Jersey coast, erosion on, 234–35

New York harbor, 17–20

Newton, Isaac, 83

Nuclear explosions, tsunamis from, 119–21

O'Brien, Morrough P., 31, 74–76, 174, 223, 249

Oceans: depth of, 6; formation of, 4–6; tides in, 90

Oil on sea surface, 60–61

Orbital motion and waves, 27, 36–38

Pacific coast of North America: atlas of, 183; beaches of, 15, 20, 184–85, 193–201, 203; erosion of, 213, 230–31; littoral transport of sand on, 219–23, 229–31; predominant waves on, 73; rise of, 12; surging on, 100–1; tides of, 89, 91, 92; tsunamis on, 108–11; wave refraction at Long Beach, 74–77

Pacific island beaches, 14, 185, 195, 197, 234

Panama Canal, tides and, 91

Photography in measuring waves, 131–32

Pierson, Willard J., 31, 46, 51

Pinholes in beaches, 210–11

Pocket beaches, 15, 185, 216

Porpoises, 127–28

Radioactive sand for tracing movement, 224–25

Rahman, Khalilur, 80–81

Rankine, W. J. M., 30, 39

Rayleigh, Lord, 30

Reflection of waves, 67–69; in seiches, 95–101

Refraction of waves, 70–77; longshore transport of sand and, 218–19; use of diagrams of, 73–77, 248

Rill marks, 206–7

Rip currents, 170–73

Ripples: current *vs.* oscillation, 212; periods of, 9; ripple marks and, 211–12

Rouvelle, A. de, 246

Russell, J. Scott, 29, 30, 65, 128, 164–65

Sand, 184–92; defined, 14, 186; how rock is made into, 215–17; littoral transport of, 213, 218–31; offshore-onshore motion of, 187–92, 203–4; size of, and slope of beach, 199–200; sizes of, 187. *See also* Beaches

Sand-pumping plants, 221, 224, 229–31

Santa Barbara, Calif., sand motion at, 220–23, 228

Saunders, Capt. Harold, 157

Saville, Thorndike, Jr., 225–26

Sea: choppy, 9, 43; fully developed, 9, 44–45, 51; irregularity of waves in, 45–47; oil on, 60–62; wind scales and, 48–49. *See also* Wind waves

Sea level, defined, 93

Seawalls: defined, 247; design of, 251, 255

Segregation of materials in earth's interior, 4, 6

Seiches, 95–101; causes of, 99–101

Seismic sea waves. *See* Tsunamis

Shallow-water waves, 66–81; defined, 34–35, 66; diffraction of, 69–70; height and, 36; periods of, 66; reflection of, 67–69, 95–101; refraction of (*see* Refraction of waves); storm surges, 77–81, 217; velocity and, 34–35

Shepard, F. P., 170

Ships, waves produced by, 121–26, 128–29

Shoreline, 6; defined, 13–14, 23; transport of sand along, 213, 218–31. *See also* Beaches; Erosion of shoreline

Shoreline structures, 246–56. *See also* Breakwaters; Groins

Silvester, Richard, 44

Solitary waves. *See* Foamlines

Spits, formation of, 16–20

Splashnik, 145

Steele, Mrs. Kaye, 133

Stevenson, Thomas, 30, 241, 245

Stokes, George G., 30, 39

Storm surges, 77–81; in Europe (1953), 78–79, 217

Storms: bars and, 202–3; beach erosion and, 198; breaking waves in, 54–55; measurement of waves in, 56–59; sea descriptions in, 49

Sun and tides, 84, 86–88

Surf, 1–2, 158–65; surveying in, 173–83

Surf beat, 166–67; periods of, 9, 166–67

Surf zones, 2; rip currents in, 170–73; types of, 163–

Surf zones (*cont'd*) 64; "undertow" in, 167–70, 173

Surfing, 126–29; of dukws, 127, 179–81

Surging, 100–1; surf beat and, 167

Surveying in the surf, 173–83

Sverdrup, Harald U., 31, 45

Swash (upwash), 204–6 210–11

Swell, 62–65; defined, 62; force of, 148; periods of, 9, 62–63; as shallow-water waves, 67; in storms, 57; velocity of, 63–65

Tetrapods, 252–54

Texas towers, 147

Thorade, H., 31

Tidal bores, 93–95

Tidal currents, 92–93

Tidal prisms in bays, 249–50

Tidal waves. *See* Storm surges; Tsunamis

Tide gauges, 133–39

Tides, 82–95; bars created by, 202; cause of, 3–4, 83–88; defined, 82; height and character of, 88–93; high and low, 83; in oceans, 90; periods of, 9, 82; rill marks and, 206–7; spring and neap, 86–88; "storm," 77; wave length of, 83

Trains of waves. *See* Swell

Tsunamis, 102–21; causes of, 103–4; defined, 3; ex-amples of, 105–11, 116–17; explosion-generated, 117–21; origin of word, 102; periods of, 9, 104; seiching from, 99–101; as shallow-water waves, 67; velocity of, 105; warning systems for, 111–16

Tucker, M. J., 145

"Undertow," 167–70, 173

Uprush (swash), 204–6, 210–11

Utah Beach, 193, 196

Van Dorn, William G., 121, 153

Velox wave system, 123–25

Volcano-generated tsunamis, 117–19

Washington, George, 214

Wave channels (tanks), 28–33; formation of bars in, 190; making waves in, 149–57

Wave crests: in breaking waves, 54–55; defined, 8; oil and, 60–61; wave height and, 35–36

Wave forecasting: for amphibious operations, 45; energy spectra and, 50–51; of storm surges, 78; of tsunamis, 111–16; of wave groups, 65

Wave fronts: measurement of, 135, 145–46; in refraction diagrams, 73–76; of tsunamis, 105

Wave groups, 64–65

Wave height: defined, 8; in destruction of lighthouses, 111, 237–39; height of berm and, 198–99; measurement of, 134; oil and other materials and, 60–62; in seas, 47; statistical observations of, 50; of tsunamis, 104–5

Wave hindcasts, 73–76; in locating structures, 248

Wave length: defined, 8; equation for, 33; of storm waves, 57; of swell, 63; of tides, 83; of tsunamis, 105

Wave measurement, 130–49; instruments for, 131–49, 245–46; of storm waves, 56–59; for tsunamis, 112–15; of wave force, 146–49, 245–46

Wave period: classification of waves by, 9; defined, 8; of shallow-water waves, 66; of swell, 62–63; in storms, 59; of tides, 9, 82; wave length and, 33

Wave steepness, 35–36; defined, 190; motion of sand and, 190–92, 226

Wave troughs, defined, 8

Wave velocity: equation for, 34–35, 63, 105; measurement of, 135; of swell, 63–65; of tsunamis, 105

Waves, 24–183; complex patterns of, 9–11, 24–25,

45–47; definition of terms for, 8; fundamental theory of, 33–41; history of research on, 27–33; mass transport in, 38–40; orbital motion and, 27, 36–38; prime natural causes of, 3–4; produced by ships, 121–26, 128–29; spectrum of, 7–9; transport of sand by, 187–92, 203–4, 213, 218–31. See also Beaches; Breaking waves; Energy of waves; Shallow-water waves; Seiches; Surf; Tides; Tsunamis; Wind waves

Waves of translation. See Foamlines

Weber brothers, 28–29, 30, 37

Whitemarsh, Lieut. Cmdr. R. P., 58–59

Wiegel, Robert, 35, 155, 255

Wind velocity: scale for, 48–49; wave spectra and, 51–53

Wind waves, 3, 42–65; breaking vs. non-breaking waves, 54–55; energy spectra and, 50–53; growth of, 42–44; oil on, 60–62; size of, 44–45. See also Shallow-water waves; Swell

"Zippering" effect, 69